Know Thyself!

Ye Are the Temple of God

Know Thyself!

Ye Are the Temple of God

Indrasen Dongre

ISPCK

Impacting Communities since 1710

2011

Know Thyself! Ye Are the Temple of God - Published by the Rev. Dr. Ashish Amos of the Indian Society for Promoting Christian Knowledge (ISPCK), Post Box 1585, 1654, Madarsa Road, Kashmere Gate, Delhi-110006 .

ISBN: 978-81-8465-154-6

Laser typeset by

ISPCK, Post Box 1585, 1654, Madarsa Road, Kashmere Gate, Delhi-110006 • *Tel:* 23866323

e-mail: ashish@ispck.org.in • ella@ispck.org.in
website: www.ispck.org.in

Contents

Foreword

Have you ever thought about how unique a position you occupy in God's Creation? You are God's supreme creation! According to the Holy Bible, you are an abode of God's Holy Spirit!

But how much do you really know about your body, spirit and soul? Despite all our scientific and technological progress, we know only a little about our body. The areas of spirit and soul are still considered as dark areas. There is a huge lack of knowledge about these aspects of our lives.

Our soul is more important than anything else in the world. If you lose wealth, something is lost; if you lose your health, much is lost; and if you lose your soul, you lose everything. That is why Jesus warns us: "For what is a man profited, if he shall gain the whole world, and lose his own soul?" (Matt. 16:26).

The divine prophet Hosea brings God's exhortation, saying, "My people are destroyed for lack of knowledge: because thou hast rejected knowledge, I will also reject thee, that thou shalt be no priest to me: seeing thou hast forgotten the law of thy God, I will also forget thy children" (Hosea 4:6).

Having the right perspective on life is one of the keys to living a life of joy and victory. This book helps you to do just that.

Indrasen Dongre

CHAPTER 1

Are You Acquainted With Yourself?

We seldom fully know about our bodies and the true state of our health, let alone our spirit and soul. In our day-to-day life, we are guided by our habits, normal schedule and physical requirements like hunger, thirst and sleep. Most of these usual activities take up most of our time, and we remain nearly oblivious of several other vital aspects of our life. Bertrand Russell observed that people carry out most of their activities just out of habit; they rarely take full advantage of their intelligence.

But man is a rational animal and is superior in intelligence to animals. Man is also superior to a supercomputer because he is not just a mechanical entity.

For thou hast made him a little lower than the angels, and hast crowned him with glory and honour.
Thou madest him to have dominion over the works of thy hands; thou hast put all [things] under his feet:
All sheep and oxen, yea, and the beasts of the field;

The fowl of the air, and the fish of the sea, [and whatsoever]
passeth through the paths of the seas.

Psalm 8:5-8

Is our ignorance about ourselves excusable? One of my relatives did not care much about his health. He was dead against the idea of going to hospital or seeing a doctor. One day, he was traveling by bus. During the journey, he had a severe heart attack. A couple of men seated next to him noticed his convulsions and his drooping head. They raised an alarm, asking the bus-driver to stop the bus. But my relative was dead by the time the bus came to a stop. His ignorance-is-bliss attitude proved fatal to him.

Our mortal and fragile bodies are the dwelling place of our immortal soul and, most astoundingly, of the Holy Spirit. Isaiah and Apostle Paul confirm this spiritual secret in the following verses:

> For thus saith the high and loft one that inhabited eternity; whose name in Holy; I dwell in the high and holy place, with him also that is of a contrite and humble spirit, to revive the heart of the contrite ones. (Isa. 57:15).

> Know ye not that ye are the temple of God; and that the spirit of God dwelleth in you? If any man defile the temple of God, him shall God destroy, which temple you are. (1 Cor. 3:16-17).

Dr. Harold J. Morobitz, Bio-Physic, Yale University, U.S.A., revealed the intrinsic value of the human body in 1970. When Dr. Morobitz undertook research in order to find out the material worth of the human body, he concluded that the estimated worth could be around $ 1,000,000,000,000,000! Remember that this research was carried out decades ago! The estimated worth would be much more today. The human body is, in fact, invaluable. The "breath of life" that God breathed into the nostrils of Adam cannot be measured in terms of money.

Blood Is Life of Flesh

Blood is life. The Bible revealed this truth over 3,000 years ago! But the world, in general, discovered this fact about 200-250 years ago! The Bible says, "And whatsoever man there be of the house of Israel or of the strangers that sojourn among you, that eateth any manner of blood, I will even set my face against that soul that eateth blood, and will cut him off from among his people. For the life of the flesh is in the blood; and I have given it to you upon the altar to make an atonement for the soul" (Lev. 17:10-11).

The internal fat, along with the blood, is regarded as the seat of life; it possesses a peculiar sanctity. It must, therefore, never be eaten by men, but always offered to God by burning (Exod. 23:18, 29:13; Lev. 3:16-17; 22-27; 17:10-16).

It was in the 18th century that William Harvey explained the importance of blood. Amazingly, what William Harvey found through his research on blood simply endorsed what the Bible says about blood.

What is most surprising to know is that Greek thinkers and philosophers, who were generally regarded as scientists, believed that blood helped "keep the head cool and calm." Owing to gross ignorance, secular people, until the time of William Harvey, carried out dangerous practices like cutting veins to let the blood of the patient flow in order to get rid of a disease or diseases. Had the world learnt from the Bible, so many veins would not have been cut open.

CHAPTER 2

Human Image in God's Likeness

The Bible says, "And God said, Let us make man in our image, after our likeness: ... So God created man in his [own] image, in the image of God created he him; male and female created he them (Gen. 1:26-27)

"And God blessed them, and God said unto them, Be fruitful, and multiply, and replenish the earth, and subdue it: and have dominion over the fish of the sea, and over the fowl of the air, and over every living thing that moveth upon the earth" (Gen. 1:28).

The above verse shows how God began to bestow His love on man by delegating certain power to His supreme creation. He gave man full dominion over all other living creatures on earth. Phrases like "in our image" and "after our likeness" emphasise the fact that man is more precious in the eyes of God than all other creatures.

Moreover, "God breathed into their nostrils the breath of life ..." when He made them! It has not happened in the case of any other living being. Evidently, God looks upon mankind alone as worthy of His fellowship and communication. As a result of these special favours, man has developed the ability to speak or communicate his thoughts and feelings.

The unique qualities of man have helped him build mighty civilisations in various parts of the world. But man's tendency to rebel against God, which is exemplified in his attempt at constructing the tower of Babel, has displeased God immensely.

What Does Likeness Mean?

Man's "likeness" to his Creator means God's unfathomable love for all. This likeness lies in the mental and moral qualities that man has—qualities such as reason, personality, free will and, above all, ability to communicate with God. Moreover, God's act of breathing the breath of life into man's nostrils links man's soul to immortality. All these amazing qualities enable man—and *only* man—to stand in special relation to God.

But God's "good" creation has a "freakish" aspect as well. The sixth chapter of Genesis speaks about "giants" among men.

> And it came to pass when men began to multiply on the face of the earth, and daughters were born to them, that the sons of God saw the daughters of men, that they were fair; and they took wives for themselves of all whom they chose…There were giants on the earth in those days, and also afterwards, when the sons of God came in to the daughters of men, and they bore children to them. Those were the mighty men who were of old, men of renown (Gen. 6:1-2 & 4).

The Bible also talks about "giants" in the Old Testament book of Numbers.

> And there we saw the giants, the sons of Anak, [which come] of the giants: and we were in our own sight as grasshoppers, and so we were in their sight (Num. 13:33).

Wickedness Invites Destruction

According to the Bible, man's wickedness called for destruction: "And God saw that the wickedness of man [was] great in the earth, and [that] every imagination of the thoughts of his heart [was] only evil continually. And it repented the Lord that he had made man on the earth, and it grieved him at his heart. And the Lord said, I will destroy man whom I have created from the face of the earth; both man, and beast, and the creeping thing, and the fowls of the air; for it repenteth me that I have made them" (Gen. 6:5-7). As a result of God's decision, the universal flood, which is described in Genesis chapter 7 and 8, destroyed all living creatures except Noah's family and the creatures in Noah' ark. The descendents of Noah's three sons later multiplied and filled the earth. But they were not better than the pre-flood people (Gen. 7-8).

After some time, God called Abram and said to him, "Get thee out of thy country, and from thy kindred, and from thy father's house, unto a land that I will shew thee" (Gen. 12:1-2). In the course of time, it came to pass that the cities of Sodom and Gomorrah were destroyed by God owing to their depravity, lascivious and filthiness. This was the second destruction after the flood in the days of Noah: "Then the Lord rained upon Sodom and upon Gomorrah brimstone and fire from the Lord out of heaven; And he overthrew those cities, and all the plain, and all the inhabitants of the cities, and that which grew upon the ground" (Gen. 19:24-25).

Even the Israelites, the chosen people of God, were no exception to vices and viciousness. Apostle Paul refers to this in his letter to Romans: "For this cause God gave them up unto vile affections: for even their women did change the natural use into that which is against nature: And likewise also the men, leaving the natural use of the woman, burned in their lust one toward another; men with men working that which is unseemly, and receiving in themselves that recompence of their error which was meet" (Rom. 1:26-27).

Brotherhood vs. Slavery

Despite the Ten Commandments given by God through Moses, mankind failed to understand the true meaning of brotherhood. The Original Sin had brought ruin, bankruptcy and spiritual poverty to the human race. For sin destroys liberty! Man's disregard to God's will in the form of sin and transgression led mankind to "slavery" — slavery in both the literal and figurative senses. And so man sold himself to the wages of sin and came under debt of the law.

Not only the Gentiles, but also the Jews were victims of this debt of the law. Evil social practices were so inevitable that the Bible, advocating fair justice and equality, had to lay down laws concerning the custom of slavery among the Hebrews:

- Extreme Poverty (Lev.), which granted liberty to sell himself

- Father selling his children (Exod. 21:7); another one selling his or her liberty

- Bankruptcy of a person (2 Kings 4:1); transgression causes a loss of man's liberty; a bankrupt man might become a servant to his creditor

- A thief unable to pay restitution (Exod. 22:2-4): "If a thief be found breaking up...; if he have nothing, then he shall be sold for his theft.

The verses in Exod. 21:1-2 and Deut. 15:12-18 exhort that the Hebrew servant who serves for six years is entitled to be freed in the seventh year, and in order to give fair justice to the slave, the master should not let him go way empty..."

Help—Mate—Women

In most communities women do not fare any better than "hidden" slaves. On the one hand, women are regarded as the fairer sex; they are lauded, even gloried among many religions as goddesses. On the other hand, there is no limit to the atrocities committed against them. In fact, women are subjected to the hidden kind of slavery. Otherwise, what explanation can humanity offer to the worldwide polygamous practice? Strangely enough, there have been exceptions to this. There have been some communities in which polyandry has been practiced, particularly the Eastern part of the world.

Male atrocities continue everywhere, whether the woman is married or widowed. No wonder, women are, by and large, considered "sex-kitten." As in the past, so also in the present, the vicious flesh trade plagues mankind.

The grand slam to this age-old malady came at the time of the advent of our Lord. Virgin Mary was hailed as the blessed one, chosen by god Almighty to launch His great plan of salvation of mankind, in the fullness of time, over a couple of thousand years ago; seemingly cursed, the clan of Eve was enhanced for the lofty spiritual task.

Jesus always treated both women and publicans well, often in the face of bitter opposition of self-righteous Jewish religious leaders like the Pharisees and scribes. He also openly criticised them for their exploitation of the widows. St. Luke makes a significant note in his Gospel about the devout women who helped our Lord and his disciples during his public ministry.

St. Luke says, "And it came to pass afterward, that he went throughout every city and village, preaching and shewing the glad tidings of the kingdom of God: and the twelve [were] with him, And certain women, which had been healed of evil spirits and infirmities, Mary called Magdalene, out of whom went seven devils, And Joanna the wife of Chuza Herod's steward, and Susanna, and many others, which ministered unto him of their substance" (Luke 8:1-3).

Besides these verses, there are several instances in which mention is made of women reacting to our Lord in great reverence in public and on both the occasions of his crucifixion and resurrection at his tomb.

However, although apostle Paul seemed to be opposed to women "speaking" in the assemblies of the Church (1 Cor. 14:34-36 and 1 Tim. 2:11-12), contrary to what he wrote in his two letters, he realised the women's power in evangelising missionary journeys that followed one after the other.

During all his three missionary journeys in Asia and Europe, he did not only welcome co-operation of devout and righteous women, but also expressed His gratitude to a number of them who substantially contributed to the success of his untiring efforts. Among them there were dynamic women such as Pricilla, Lydia, Thyathira, Tabitha, Phoebe (called our sister by him), Mary, Thryphen, Tryphasa and Persis.

Apostle Paul is probably cautious for the following three main reasons:

- Man was created before woman, who was a help-mate for him.

- Woman was the first transgressor, showing that she yielded more readily to temptation.

- The ancient world was male-dominated.

Nevertheless, the Bible never showed any partiality in portraying women as they really were from the very first-ever couple of Adam and Eve down to the women of substance and real guts in the Old Testament and the New Testament.

In olden times, women were regarded as mere "shadows." However, in the Old Testament, we get to read about some remarkable women, such as Sarah, Rebecca and Rachael, whose work and contributions were substantial. In Exod. 2:9 and 15:21 and Numbers chapter 12, we learn that Miriam, the sister of Moses, was a prophetess.

And in times of the Judges, Deborah looked after the responsibility of a Judge (Judg. chapters 4-5). Moabite Ruth proved to be the most precious blessing not only to the Israelites, but also to the whole world. In Samuel 1:1 and 2:11, the righteous wife Hannah of Elkanah has no parallel in the whole of the Old Testament.

Equality of Gender

An organisation called Christians for Biblical Equality (CBE), USA, has issued its CBE mission statement in seventeen languages. In accordance with this statement, CBE emphasises that all Christian believers, without regard to gender, race, and class, are free and encouraged to use their God-given gifts in families, ministries and communities.

In its statement, CBE emphasises: "We believe in the equality and essential dignity of men and women of all ethnicities, ages and classes. We recognise that all persons are made in the image of God and are to reflect that image in the community of believers in the home and society."

CHAPTER 3

Dark Shadows of the Garden of Eden

God's creation of heaven and earth culminated in the making of man. He saw that Adam was alone among all other living creatures He had made. So He thought of making a suitable help for Adam. God made Eve and brought her to Adam. He was pleased to see Eve and said, "This is now bone of my bones and flesh of my flesh; Eve shall be called woman, because she was taken out of man, for God intended that they shall be man and his wife" (Gen. 2:15-25).

With the creation of the first couple—Adam and Eve—God founded the human family in the Garden of Eden. And he blessed them, saying, "... be fruitful and multiply, and replenish the earth, and subdue it ..." (Gen. 1:28). He also gave them some commands for safety and security. But it was left to them to choose whether to abide by them or risk their life, for God had warned them of the ill-effects of disobedience.

So, the first couple began to live in peace in the Garden of Eden; and they also enjoyed the fellowship of their Creator daily in the cool of the day. But we read the biblical account of the failure of Adam and Eve to keep God's first-ever command. For Satan, in the form of a serpent, engineered their fall with his crafty and cunning words. They were lured away to eat of the tree of the knowledge of good and bad, which was forbidden by God. They then lost the paradise and immortal life, besides God's fellowship.

The fall pushed Adam and Eve into the dark shadows of sin and death. Their disobedience let loose the reign of sin and death on not only the two of them, but also on their progeny and descendents. Wickedness, hatred and violence crept into their offspring when Adam and Eve gave birth to Cain and Abel: Cain murdered his younger brother, Abel. Thus says the Bible about this violent act: "The lord God had said to Cain, what hast thou done, the voice of thy brother's blood crieth unto me from the ground. And now art thou cursed from the earth which hath opened her mouth to receive thy brother's blood from thy hand" (Gen. 4:10-1).

Thus, started with Cain's act of violence against his own younger brother Abel, the brotherhood of mankind got drowned deep in bloodshed during the bygone ages and in battles and wars later.

This reminds us of what Paul wrote in one of his letters, "Wherefore, as by one man sin entered into the world, and death by sin; and so death passed upon all men, for that all have sinned" (Rom. 5:12).

Hatred, treachery and violence prevailed among the descendents of Adam and Eve. Selfishness made man forget brotherhood, and blissful married life became a rare thing. Perverted lust presented an ugly picture. In several countries, the institution of marriage has lost its meaning due to open or concealed polygamy and sodomous practices. Gays and lesbians demand their right under the nice name of individual liberty; statistics concerning the social stigma of homosexuality are illusive.

The Ten Commandments and their deeply moral version presented by Jesus in his Sermon on the Mount, stand like lighthouses, lovingly guiding mankind. Love and care constitute the foundation of marital bliss and healthy family life. Paul admonishes in one of his letters: "For, brethren, ye have been called unto liberty; only [use] not liberty for an occasion to the flesh, but by love serve one another (Gal. 5:13). Here Paul hits the nail on the head, indeed.

When man considers himself free to choose whatever he likes as an independent individual using his own ideas about how to live life and behave, he ruins himself and his family life. The classic historical instance is found in the Bible account of the two-centered civilisations, namely Sodom and Gomorrah. They were overthrown by the divine wrath in the times of Abraham and Lot (Gen. chapter 19).

The newly convert Christians in the city of Corinth had misconstrued Paul's statement, which occurred in his letter, that "all things are lawful." In certain other context (1 Cor. 10:23), confused in their minds about Paul's statement, the Corinthians began applying the principle generally to sensual indulgences, whereas Paul granted liberty in respect of meats (that is, sacrificial, idolatrous feast). The Corinthians seemed to have claimed that they were free to satisfy all their bodily desires, now that the Gospel of Jesus Christ had set them free from association of idolatry (1 Cor. 19-20).

As Christian believers, our bodies partake of the mystical union that exists between Christ and His disciples. How shameful it is, therefore, to violate this union by acts of immoral behaviour. The Christian believer is united with Christ in a spiritual union, just as the husband and the wife are "one flesh."

We must keep ourselves beyond the reach of this sin, for there is none that defiles the body like this one and makes it unfit for the Holy Spirit. When we are spiritually conscious and faced with temptations of this kind, our bodies and minds turn into a virtual battlefield.

Writing to Galatians, Paul explains how one's body and mind are a battlefield of internal spiritual warfare that goes on almost continually: For the flesh lusteth against the spirit, and the spirit against the flesh: and the things that you would .....Now the works of the flesh are adultery, fornication uncleanness, lasciviousness (Gal. 5:17-21; also, see Eph. 6:12).

The Old Testament records two major incidents that were caused by the wickedness of the people, which provoked the wrath of God and destroyed them on two different occasions:

• And God saw that the wickedness of man [was] great in the earth, and [that] every imagination of the thoughts of his heart [was] only evil continually. And it repented the Lord that he had made man on the earth, and it grieved him at his heart. And the Lord said, I will destroy man whom I have created from the face of the earth; both man, and beast, and the creeping thing, and the fowls of the air; for it repenteth me that I have made them (Gen. 6:5-8). And after, in chapters 7 and 8, this follows a detailed account of the universal flood.

• On another occasion, remembering His Covenant with Noah, God overthrew only the wicked cities of Sodom and Gomorrah, when Lot's wife was punished. (Gen. 19:23-27). Unless humans use their freewill to choose judiciously, they will not please their Creator.

Man, the most wonderful living creature created by God, is indeed the universe in miniature; Man's nervous system is simply marvelous; his brain controls the various parts of his body.

So, the Bible—both the Old Testament and the New Testament—succinctly gives guidelines on the proper and judicious use of various parts of the body, such as the eyes, the mouth, the tongue and so on. Let us take a look at what the Bible has to say for some of the important parts of the body:

The Hand
"And if thy right hand offend thee, cut it off, and cast it from thee; for it is profitable for thee that one of your members should perish, and not thy whole body should be cast into hell" (Matt. 5:29).

The Eye
"And if thy right eye offend thee, cut it off, and cast it from thee; for it is profitable for thee that one of your members should perish, and not thy whole body should be cast into hell" (Matt. 5:30).

The Tongue
Man's tongue is an ungovernable part when it comes to maintaining good relations with other persons, either in the family or in the society. While the tongue plays a major role in the act of communication, it can cause irreparable damage to our relations with other people.

In his letter, St. James warns against the tongue, saying, "And the tongue [is] a fire, a world of iniquity: so is the tongue among our members, that it defileth the whole body, and setteth on fire the course of nature; and it is set on fire of hell. For every kind of beasts, and of birds, and of serpents, and of things in the sea, is tamed, and hath been tamed of mankind: But the tongue can no man tame; [it is] an unruly evil, full of deadly poison. Therewith bless we God, even the Father; and therewith curse we men, which are made after the similitude of God.

Out of the same mouth proceedeth blessing and cursing. My brethren, these things ought not so to be" (James 3: 6-10).

James is seen here focusing on the importance of the tongue and the terrible havoc it can wreak on human relations. The truth of his words is amply confirmed by the negative effects of gossip, rumors, destructive criticism and idle words.

James' words are reminiscent of Jesus' stern warning: "That every idle word that men shall speak, they shall give account thereof in the day of judgment. For by thy words thou shalt be condemned" (Matt. 12:36-37). Therefore, he exhorts us: "But let your communication be, Yea, yea; Nay, nay: for whatsoever is more than these cometh of evil" (Matt. 5: 37).

In our efforts to discipline our tongues, it is useful to ask the following questions before we speak: Is it true? Is it necessary? Is it kind? This habit of thinking before speaking will save us from many tragic experiences, misunderstandings, enmity and broken relationships (Prof. C. N. Balderas; based on the sermon given at All Saints' Cathedral, Shillong, in 1987).

CHAPTER 4

Great Future and Hope for Mankind

The Bible gives us hope—the hope of an eternal and resurrected life in the presence of God and Lord Jesus Christ. This hope is so great that sometimes some of us find it hard to believe in the Word of God.

When Lazarus was dead and buried four days before, Jesus, "saith unto her (Martha), Thy brother shall rise again. Martha saith unto him, I know that he shall rise again in the resurrection at the last day. Jesus said unto her, I am the resurrection, and the life: he that believeth in me, though he were dead, yet shall he live" (John 11:23-25).

Man is mortal: the body returns to dust. However, death is not the final end. Great hope has been given by Jesus' death on the Cross and his resurrection on the third day. He referred to it figuratively while speaking to his disciples before his death on the Cross.

St. John has graphically recorded Jesus' words: "Verily, verily, I say unto you, except a corn of wheat fall into the ground and die, it abideth alone: but if it die, it bringeth forth much fruit" (John 12:24). "And ye now therefore have sorrow: but I will see you again, and your heart shall rejoice, and your joy no man taketh from you" (John 16:22). Jesus foretold his death on the Cross and illustrated his resurrection by raising Lazarus from the dead. His wonderful action was matched with the succinct words that he spoke while talking to Martha before divine act.

His earth-bound divine life was confined to Himself as long as He remained on earth in the body of His humiliation. But when, by His death and Resurrection, the earthly shell (body) was cast off, the way was for diffusion of the divine life among all mankind. Here, the actual seed sown does not reappear, but something higher, or the complete plant, springs from it.

When the group of Greeks, that is, Gentiles, probably from Galilee or Decapolis, sought an interview with Jesus, their request vividly brought before His mind His own approaching death on the Cross.

Here, the analogy used by Jesus has been proved literally true in a report on an excavation narrated by Dr. Henry Ward Beecher, the great clergy, while delivering his sermon: he told about an archeological discovery. The scientist found an ancient tomb in Egypt. On opening the tomb, they found inside it, kept in the company of the dead monarch, kernels of wheat that had lain there for over 3,000 years!

The discoverers sowed the kernel of wheat. And amazingly the grains of wheat, which had lain untouched for 3,000 years in the ancient tomb, produced a good harvest. With his fine oratory about man's mortality, Dr. Beecher concludes: "If wheat will keep as long as that, I am sure, man will go again."

In fact, the doctrine of resurrection and future life was not clearly revealed in olden days. It is Paul who took the thread of Jesus' analogy of the grain of wheat. Paul threw clear light on the nature of the resurrection-body. He pointed out that the bodies of redeemed believers will undergo a similar change. He based the doctrine of life after resurrection on Christ's victorious resurrection. (1 Cor. 15: 50-58).

Man's Death: Door to Eternity

According to Paul, the great hope that the Creator gives to man makes Christian believers ready for and fearless about carnal death. This hope comes as covetous and desirable in the face of the inevitability of infirmities, troubles and mortality. In his second letter to the Corinthians, Paul strives hard to approve himself to Christ, saying:

> For we know that if our earthly house of [this] tabernacle were dissolved, we have a building of God, a house not made with hands, eternal in the heavens. For in this we groan, earnestly desiring to be clothed upon with our house which is from heaven: If so be that being clothed we shall not be found naked. For we that are in [this] tabernacle do groan, being burdened: not for that we would be unclothed, but clothed upon, that mortality might be swallowed up of life. Now he that hath wrought us for the selfsame thing [is] God, who also hath given unto us the earnest of the Spirit. Therefore [we are] always confident, knowing that, whilst we are at home in the body, we are absent from the Lord: (For we walk by faith, not by sight) We are confident, [I say] and willing rather to be absent from the body, and to be present with the Lord. Wherefore we labour, that, whether present or absent, we may be accepted of him. For we must all appear before the judgment seat of Christ; that every one may receive the things [done] in [his] body, according to that he hath done, whether [it be] good or bad. (2 Cor. 5:1-10)

> Therefore if any man [be] in Christ, [he is] a new creature: old things are passed away; behold, all things are become

new. And all things [are] of God, who hath reconciled us
to himself by Jesus Christ, and hath given to us the
ministry of reconciliation. (2 Cor. 5:17-18)

Paul's explanation found in the first letter to the Corinthians,
therefore, stands firm like a unique lighthouse, showing what
kind of resurrection-bodies are to be:

But some [man] will say, How are the dead raised up?
and with what body do they come? [Thou] fool, that which
thou sowest is not quickened, except it die: And that which
thou sowest, thou sowest not that body that shall be, but
bare grain, it may chance of wheat, or of some other grain
But God giveth it a body as it hath pleased him, and to
every seed his own body. All flesh [is] not the same flesh:
but [there is] one [kind of] flesh of men, another flesh of
beasts, another of fishes, [and] another of birds. [There
are] also celestial bodies, and bodies terrestrial: but the
glory of the celestial [is] one, and the [glory] of the
terrestrial [is] another. [There is] one glory of the sun, and
another glory of the moon, and another glory of the stars:
for [one] star differeth from [another] star in glory. So also
[is] the resurrection of the dead. It is sown in corruption;
it is raised in incorruption (1 Cor 15:35-42)

Foretelling Events

The following major events in Jesus' earthly life indicate the
inscrutability of divine ways:

- Christ—the resurrection and the life. This is foretold in his
  great miracle of raising of Lazarus to life as narrated by St.
  John in his Gospel (chapter 11)

- Jesus' transfiguration on Mount Hermon near Caesarea
  Philippi, (Matt. 17: 1-9; Mark 9:2-9 and Luke 9:28-36)

- Resurrected Jesus vindicated the glorified, that is,
  redemption-bodies of Christian believers at Jesus' second
  coming in the universal resurrection.

Most significantly, the above-mentioned events are closely linked to one another: While Jesus' transfiguration on Mount Hermon establishes His Divine Sonship, His raising of Lazarus from the dead to life shows that Christ is the resurrection and the life; and His own resurrection on the third day illustrates His saints' gloried, redemption-bodies at his second advent, *like those of Moses and Elijah* (1 Cor. 15:1-58).

What is most striking is that the knowledge of this particular event was to be withheld at the instructions of Jesus until His crucifixion in Jerusalem. So, the three disciples accompanying Him on Mount Hermon remained silent. The sect of Sadducees did not believe in either resurrection or the concept of life after death; similarly, some of the Corinthians too did believe the fact of the dead, and apparently, that of Jesus Christ as well.

This occasioned Paul to write chapter 15 concerning resurrection and redemption-bodies. In verses 22-23, he says: "For as in Adam all die, even so in Christ shall all be made alive. But every man in his own order: Christ the first fruits; afterward they that are Christ's at his coming."

Then the apostle almost rebukes here that the denial of the resurrection of the dead logically leads to the denial of Christ's Resurrection, thus overwhelming the whole of Christian faith (1 Cor. 15: 20-28).

Moreover, Paul explains in this letter to the Corinthians how Jesus' resurrection had significant consequences on Christ life and practice. Each one of these consequences could be considered a milestone in spiritual history (1 Cor. 15:20-28).

Furthermore, the apostle throws light on the nature of the seed and the plant by using the analogy of Jesus (1 Cor. 15:35-44).

He reminds the Corinthians of the differences that exist between bodies of various living creatures, other than men. So the resurrected body will spring from the earthly one, and it will be more glorious—a spiritual body, not like Adam's earthly body, but like the body of the resurrected Christ (1 Cor. 15:45-49)

Fully Manifest Now

The ignorance that existed during the olden times about this vital subject has been fully wiped out; it is fully manifested now:

- Jesus' Resurrection has changed what was previously partially revealed into a "sure and certain hope" (2 Tim. 1:10).

- Paul advises Christian believers about walking in the newness of life after baptism, in the mystical union with Jesus (Rom. 6: 4).

- It is a pledge that we too shall rise (from the dead) again. (2 Cor. 4:16; Rom. 8:11).

- It was the real body of the resurrected Christ bearing the marks of His former "natural body" (John 20:27).

- The body was capable of receiving food (Luke 24:43).

- The resurrected body of Christ was recognised by those who had formerly known Him, apparently only when He willed to be recognised; yet it could be transported mysteriously from place to place, passing even through closed doors.

Glorified and Natural Body

We may infer that the glorified body will have some relation to the natural body, thus preserving personal identity, but laid to rest; it will be free from its limitations and imperfections, a fit abode for the perfect spirit. The Resurrection of our Lord is the final triumph over sin and death.

The appearance of Moses and Elijah is, obviously, Moses representing the Law, Elijah representing the prophets and our Saviour working as seen in their midst—greater than both.

Christ is the end of law (Rom. 10:4) besides the object to which all prophecy pointed (Luke 24: 44, 28: 23; Rom. 3:21); that therefore the great purpose of these had now been fulfilled; and that, after their testimony thus given, Moses and Elijah disappear, while Jesus alone remains.

CHAPTER 5

Human Body and Mind

People today seem to have assumed more importance than ever before in society. And that is because the days of monarch, royalty and serfdom are over. The turbulent current of commercialisation and democratic trends and the era of human rights have enhanced the significance of the individual. The consumer is the king.

Advertising agencies spare no pains to find customers and end-users through media like the newspaper, the television and the radio. In this situation, where efforts are being made to usher in a liberal society, depravity adds fuel to the fire!

In big cities, young boys and girls coming from affluent families are readily attracted to pubs, night-clubs, dancing bars and what have you. These fashion-conscious boys and girls are easily drawn to the showy world of modeling, fashion and showbiz.

Stress and Strain

There is yet another section of society that has to deal with the daily grind of work, errands and never-ending responsibilities.

This large section of men and women has to cope with a lot of stress and strain. And so they crave for relaxation.

A newspaper carried a two-part ad write-up, saying: "HOW SPA THERAPIES HELP YOU TO RELAX!" It urged the victims of stress to pay a visit to a "five-fountain spa" to combat the effects of stress with the help of a relaxing massage.

But do these spas really deliver the goods—that is the question. Thousands of years ago, the Holy Bible prescribed the best remedy to this problem, saying: "Commit thy way unto the Lord, trust also in him; and he shall bring it to pass" (Ps. 37:5).

In his book, *Human Destiny*, Lecomte du Nouy, evolutionist, says: It is clear that God abdicated a portion of His omnipotence, when he gave man the liberty of choices. Man— according to the second chapter of Genesis and our hypothesis— possesses a real independence... It is no longer the strongest, the most agile, the physically fittest, who must survive, but the most morally evolved. The new supremacy can only manifest itself if man is free to choose his path. This is, therefore, an apparent limitation of omnipotence of the Creator, consented by him in order to bestow freedom upon the chosen species, so as to impose a final test. Having been bestowed with conscience, man acquired an independence of which he must show himself to be worthy, under pain of regressing toward the best (Adapted from *Human Destiny*, Nouy, Page 139, Signet Book, The New American Library, Inc., 245, Fifth Avenue, New York, N.Y., U.S.A.)

The Bible says: "For as he thinketh in his heart, so is he..." (Prov. 23:7). How you think can powerfully impact your feelings and how you live. This intimate link between the mind and the body is a vital secret of human life. What affects the mind, affects the body and vice versa. Man's physical and spiritual welfare is based on the function of the mind. God has given tools and techniques so as to pave the way for the mind to change and improve one's behaviour and health.

It is indeed rather sad that man has not been able to gain control over his mind. Man's mind is a very complex part of his personality. It is closely linked with the sensory organs, which get easily dominated by man's bodily tendencies. His failure to control or supervise the complex process of their joint operation leads him to make the mistake that Adam and Eve made years ago.

Man's dominion of his spirit solely rests with God. It calls forth in its possessor feelings of weakness, unworthiness and impurity. Man lives with an uneasy conscience—almost naked before the Creator. This is where Christian faith comes to man's rescue. It ultimately brings about a reconciliation between man and God.

Paul exhorts the Galatians to "stand fast therefore in the liberty wherewith Christ hath made us free, and be not entangled again with the yoke of bondage" (Gal. 5:11).

And the Old Testament promise surpasses the expectations of the young and the old. It gives a sure remedy for physical and mental problems such as stress, strain and exhaustion. This remedy is revealed by God through His servant prophet Isaiah:

> Hast thou not known? Hast thou not heard that the everlasting God, the Lord, the Creator of the ends of the earth, fainteth not, neither is weary? There is no searching of his understanding. He giveth power to the faint; and to them that have no might he increaseth strength. Even the youths shall faint and be weary, and the young men shall utterly fall (Isa. 40:28-30).

Is Man Part Machine?

Studies have shown that exercise reduces anxiety, stress and depression. Exercise strengthens one's body. It triggers the brain's release of endorphins, which help relieve and boost mood. And the best result comes when we exercise regularly five to six times a week. Drinking plenty of water and/or fruit juices improves the body, especially the digestive system.

Some scientists talk about a futurist man who can beat biological limitations by becoming part-machine! Inventor and futurist Ray Kurzwell[1] is reported to have said that he expects that in a couple of decades, humans would routinely incorporate machines in their bodies. He said that human endeavours are supplemented with technology to a large degree already.

Kurzwell cites examples of computer and technological advancement and remarks that it is time we stopped believing our fears and superstitious beliefs and embraced technological innovation aimed at advancing human civilisation beyond current physical limits.

Countering the view, Rupa Sengupta[2] raises many ethical and logical questions:

- Must we deny humanity itself?

- Should mastery of nature mean death of nature?

- Do we really want a synthetic perfect world in which boredom kills instead of malady?

- Do we want supercomputers for friends or cyborgs as lovers who don't snore or dream?

---

[1] Ray Kurzwell is chancellor of a new institutions. Singularity University meant to study advances in biotechnology, robotics and genetics.

[2] "Times—View and Counter View" by Rupa Sengupta, *The Times of India*, Pune, 14 February, 2009.

She points out that humans are humans because they are born, they age and they die. Loving and hating, they know happiness, fear and pain. Biologically bound yet free agents, they vacillate and choose. Through it all, they realise that death and finitude can only be overcome intellectually.

Man's struggle against frailty is, therefore, spiritual; and that is where human achievement lies. So, let's stop making Faustian pacts with singularity, the point where natural laws break down.

CHAPTER 6

Healthy Mind, Body and Society

Exercise for the Heart

As we know, the heart is one of the most vital parts of our body and the less strenuously it works the longer it lasts. Those with sedentary jobs are more susceptible to heart diseases than those with active, physical jobs. But not many of us know that running mercy-based errands for Jesus can really improve the condition of our heart. (From *The Last Day Watchmen*, Vol. 4, No. 1 June 2008/SAD-26). Some research findings state that disease will never be cured or eradicated by only the present materialistic methods for the simple reason that disease in its origin is not material.

Age-old adages such as "Heath is wealth" and "a healthy mind in a healthy body" lay stress on the fact that man's mind and body are co-related. This implies that diseases are not merely material in nature; most of them are related to the mind. Disease is in essence the result of the conflicts between the soul and the mind. It cannot be fully eradicated except by spiritual and mental efforts.

"Such efforts can cure and prevent disease by removing those basic factors which are its primary cause. No effort directed to the body alone can do more than superficially repair damage, and in this there is no cure, since the cause is still operative and may at any moment again demonstrate its presence in another form... "(From *Heal Thyself* by Edward A. Bach; excerpts: *Time of India*, 28 January 2009).

Edward Bach says that "disease may be prevented before its onset—or aborted in its earlier stage—if proper corrective spiritual and mental efforts are undertaken."

The Bible goes deeper than any available explanation about man's illness when it categorically states:

> Wherefore, as by one man sin entered into the world, and death by sin; and so death passed upon all men, for that all have sinned: (For until the law sin was in the world: but sin is not imputed when there is no law. Nevertheless death reigned from Adam to Moses, even over them that had not sinned after the similitude of Adam's transgression, who is the figure of him that was to come (Rom. 5:12-14).

Whatever the state of the world has been before the advent of Jesus, it became clear that He came as the "light of the world." Isaiah had foretold about it over seven hundred years before: Then shall thy light break forth as the morning and thine health shall spring forth speedily and thy righteousness shall go before thee, the glory of the Lord shall be thy reward" (Isa. 58:8).

In the first 1 to 7 verses of this chapter (Isa. 58:1-7), fasting and praying of the Israelites analyse the shortcomings, clearly showing their sins of omission, disapproving the kind of fasts they observe.

Divine Protection
When Jesus, the light of the world, came to the world, the above-mentioned promises were fulfilled. The only sinless, holy and

perfect person of Jesus died a sacrificial death on the Cross to atone for the sins of the world. Jesus brought light and health with Him as divine protection to Christian believers.

The gospels shed ample light on how the public ministry of Jesus came as fulfillment of the prophecy through His healing the sick, casting out evil spirits, giving the blind sight and raising the dead from the dead. Satan has been restless: evil powers and rulers of darkness are at work in the world.

How can the prince of darkness sit idle when Jesus defeated death on the Cross and rose again as the first fruit among the dead? He has been bent upon destroying the witness of the true believers and taking the last vestige of morality, decency and spirituality. The Bible says that our enemy and his accomplices are powerful. It describes Satan as an enemy of God and clearly warns Christian believers against Satan: "Be sober, be vigilant, because your adversary the devil, as a roaring lion, walketh about seeking whom he may devour."

Craze for Physical Fitness

People all over the world are becoming more and more health conscious. Medical care is also improving by leaps and bounds. Medical research has also quelled man's fear of quite a few seemingly incurable diseases. Besides, many have started taking an active interest in sports to keep fit and fine. Many have also begun to see the importance of self-discipline and self-regulation. As a result, life expectancy in many countries has grown.

Although scientists and researchers have contributed much towards enabling people to lead healthier lives, they still need to stay away from conducting researches just to satisfy their curiosity; for example, researches directed at creating test-tube babies (surrogate mothers), cloning of animals and humans, etc. Scientific research must be carried out with the purpose of meeting the needs of society. Knowledge that does not contribute to social welfare is useless knowledge.

Man must not ignore what the Bible says on this subject: "For we must appear before the judgment seat of Christ: that every one may receive the things done in his body, according to that he hath done whether it be good or bad" (2 Cor. 5:10).

Healthy Society

We all have utopian ideals. But most of us do not know how to realise our ideals. Let us take a look at what the Bible has to say on the quest for a perfect world. John the Baptist invited people to repent, proclaiming that the Kingdom of God was at hand. After his important ministry came to an end, Jesus declared that the Kingdom of God or Kingdom of Heaven was at hand. He spoke more boldly and authoritatively than John.

Then before His sacrificial death on the Cross, Jesus promised Peter to establish His Church on his divinely-inspired faith. And after His death, resurrection and ascension, His Church was founded in Jerusalem on the Pentecost Day, when the Holy Spirit, in the form of a tongue of fire, came and settled on each one of those who had gathered to pray. And it was Peter who was leading the worship in the Upper Room! This was the first Church.

The Church is a divine institution the members of which are chosen and set apart as Christian believers, some of whom are saved and some are in the process of being saved by the grace of God (2 Cor. 5:17).

Thus, the Church as the body of Christ could be nearer to the ideal community of believers. In fact, the Church marks the new beginning of the Kingdom of Heaven among humans, who had lost Paradise after the fall of Adam and Eve.

Church members are in the various stages of salvation and sanctification. Nevertheless, the Church of Christ constitutes the Family of God. For each one of them stands a witness to the gospel of Christ. As ambassadors for Him, they are engaged in the spread of the Kingdom of God. Consisting of the Jews and the Gentiles, the Church could be regarded as the new Israel, liberated from the bondage of sin and fear of death, as they are justified as righteous through their faith in Jesus the Saviour.

While Christian believers are freed from the obligation of the Mosaic laws of ceremonies, they are still bound, more than ever (Rom. chapter 6), to "the obedience of the commandments which are called moral ones."

Sermon on the Mount

What did Jesus do with the Ten Commandments? To find this out, let us take a look at His famous "Sermon on the Mount":

- He summed up the Ten Commandments under the obligations to love God and to love our neighbours, for these two obligations are the two sides of the law of universal love ("Love is the fulfilling of the law").

- Our Lord widened and deepened the scope of the Ten Commandments, making them applicable to outward act and to the inner spirit and motive.

- He changed them from being mere negative commands to abstain from sins to being positive obligations, which are never exhausted and involve a perpetual advance in holiness, where mere abstention from evil acts implies moral stagnation.

Thus, the Church as the body of Christ after his ascension constitutes the army of Christian believers who continue to combat Satan's forces of darkness and continue to work for the spread of the Kingdom of God. Jesus said, "The Kingdom is within you" (Luke 17:21). What is this Kingdom of God or Kingdom of Heaven like?

In his book, Isaiah draws a brief sketch of it:

That he who blesseth himself in the earth shall bless himself in the God of truth; and he that sweareth in the earth shall swear by the God of truth; because the former troubles are forgotten, and because they are hid from mine eyes (Isa. 65:16).

But be ye glad and rejoice for ever [in that] which I create: for, behold, I create Jerusalem a rejoicing, and her people a joy. And I will rejoice in Jerusalem, and joy in my people: and the voice of weeping shall be no more heard in her, nor the voice of crying (Isa. 65:18-19).

They shall not build, and another inhabit; they shall not plant, and another eat: for as the days of a tree [are] the days of my people, and mine elect shall long enjoy the work of their hands. They shall not labour in vain, nor bring forth for trouble; for they [are] the seed of the blessed of the LORD, and their offspring with them (Isa. 65:22-23).

And it shall come to pass, that before they call, I will answer; and while they are yet speaking, I will hear. The wolf and the lamb shall feed together, and the lion shall eat straw like the bullock: and dust [shall be] the serpent's meat. They shall not hurt nor destroy in all my holy mountain, saith the Lord (Isa 65:24-25).

We get an insight into the Heavenly Kingdom in the New Testament book of Matthew as well:

At the same time came the disciples unto Jesus, saying, 'Who is the greatest in the kingdom of heaven?' And Jesus called a little child unto him, and set him in the midst of them, and said, 'Verily I say unto you, except ye be converted, and become as little children, ye shall not enter into the kingdom of heaven. Whosoever therefore shall humble himself as this little child, the same is greatest in the kingdom of heaven. And who so shall receive one such little child in my name receiveth me' (Matt.18:1-5).

Parables concerning the Kingdom of Heaven:

- Parable of Mustard Seed (Matt. 13:37-43)

- Parable of Leaven(Matt. 13:33)

- Parables of Mustard Tare (Matt. 13:37-43)

- Parable of Godly Pearls (Matt. 13: 45-46)

- Parable of Net (Matt. 23:47-49)

CHAPTER 7

Myth of Conflicts between Science and the Bible

A ll wisdom and knowledge flow from God. God alone is the sole source of life, purity or holiness and all good things of life. The Bible is the Word of God. It is through the Bible that He reveals not only Himself, but also the things to come. He does so because He loves mankind, which he created in his own image and likeness. In brief, God created the universe and man gave birth to science, art, philosophy, architecture and the like.

Genesis: Focal Point

Some individuals from the scientific community raised questions and doubts about the authenticity of the Old Testament book of Genesis. Some of them happened to be atheists. Their attitudes and works show that scientific research tends to oppose the Bible. Their views end up in creating the impression that science and the Bible contradict each other.

But not all scientists are atheists. A survey conducted by two scientists in 1996 showed that the percentage of university scientists who believed not only in God, but also a personal

God who answer prayers had remained more or less constant at around 40 per cent since 1916. (The survey made by Edward J. Larsen and Larry Withan, "Scientists are still keeping faith", Nature-386; April 1997; 433-36.)

Sir Alfred North Whitehead once observed that mediaeval Europe in 1500 A.D. knew less than Archimedes in the third-century B.C., and yet by 1700, Newton had written his masterpiece *Principia Mathematica*. Whitehead wondered how such an explosion of knowledge could happen so quickly. And his answer was: "Modern science must come from the mediaeval insistence on the rationality of God" (Alfred North Whitehead, "Science and Modern World." London, Macmillan, 1925). C. S. Lewis says, "Men became scientific because they expected law in the nature and because they believed in a Law-giver!"

In this context, we have a formidable list of eminent scientists:

- Galileo (1564-1642)

- Kepler (1571-1630)

- Pascal (1623-1662)

- Boyle (1627-1691)

- Newton (1642-1727)

- Faraday (1791-1867)

- Babbage (1792-1871)

All of the above scientists were theist, and most of them were Christian believers. Their belief in God, far from being a hindrance to their science, was often the main inspiration for it!

What is more, the Bible asserts in unambiguous terms the creative power of God:

- "And thou, Lord in the beginning hast laid the foundation of the earth; and the heavens are work of thine hands" (Heb. 1:10).

- "Of old hast thou laid the foundation of the earth and the heavens are works of thy hands" (Heb. 4:3).

Although the word "science" does not occur in the Bible, it is indeed part and parcel of its narration of all major developments—right from Creation, Fall and the Redemption plan of God for man to hope for the bright future of man. Thus, God is the only source and originator of wisdom and knowledge. Man only uses scientific means to reveal His creative acts.

Through the scientific method scientists classify their findings into various categories. But they can never boast of comprehending God's design and plan.

The following Bible verses clearly show the difference between the ways of God and those of man:

- "Seek ye the Lord while he may be found, call ye upon him while he is near...For my thoughts are not your thoughts, neither are your ways my ways, saith the Lord. For as the heavens are higher than the Earth, so are my ways higher than your ways, and my thoughts than your thoughts" (Isa. 55:6, 8-9).

- "O Lord, how great are thy works and thy thoughts are very deep" (Ps. 92:5).

- "The Lord knoweth the thoughts of man, that they are vanity" (Ps. 94:11).

Job's Story

The story of Job stands in the Bible as an account of man's inquisitiveness about God's governance of this world, about God Himself and about His Creation. In his long suffering, Job — claiming to be innocent — and his four friends discuss the cause of Job's suffering. He reproaches God for avoiding him, while his friends argue and reason out with Job as to what lay behind his tragedy and suffering.

At long last, God answers Job. In His long speech, covering chapters 38 to 41, God answers mankind, indirectly chiding even the scientist of today! God challenges Job to answer Him, while enumerating His own mighty works. He convinces Job of his ignorance, saying:

> Who is this that darkneth counsel by words without knowledge, (that is, with vain talk)? ...Where wast thou when I had laid the foundation of the earth? Declare, if thou hast understanding. Who hath laid the measures thereof, if thou knowest? Or who hath stretched the line upon it? Whereupon are the foundation thereof fastened? Or who laid the corner stone thereof... (Job. 38:1-6).

Answering Job, God said further, "Shall he that contendeth with the Almighty instruct him? He that reproveth God, let him answer it." Then Job said, "Behold, I am vile; what shall I answer thee? I will lay mine hand upon my mouth" (Job 40:1-5).

Job had brought the deserved rebuke on himself for his attack on God's rule of the world, and he needed to rise to a higher point of view from which he could see the complexity of the problem. Since the supreme lesson of the book of Job is that Job becomes so sure of God that he here knows his inabilities to be in harmony with God righteousness though he is wholly incapable of reconciling the two intellectually.

A short dialogue between God and Job ended in Job's confession and submission. Job declared that he understood God's relation to man. At once, he retracted his words and repented of all that he had said amiss. The clearer apprehension of his majesty and righteousness humbled Job to dust.

CHAPTER 8

Church—Body of Christ

The Church of Christ is said to be the new beginning of the Kingdom of God or Kingdom of Heaven for mankind after the fall of Adam and Eve in the Garden of Eden.

Meanwhile, God had implemented His plan of Salvation for mankind by Jesus' ministry, death on the Cross, Resurrection and Ascension. Jesus, God incarnate, then laid the foundation of His Church as promised during the landmark conversation He had with his disciples.

And it came to pass, after rebuking the sign-seeking Pharisees and Sadducees, Jesus and his disciples went into the coasts of Caesarea Philippi. Jesus asked them, "Whom do men say that I the Son of man am?" His disciples told Him about the different opinions people had about Him.

And when Jesus asked them, "But whom say ye that I am?" Peter said, "Thou art the Christ, the son of the living God." Pleased with his answer, Jesus said, "Blessed art thou, Simon Barjona for flesh and blood hath not revealed it unto you, but my Father in heaven, And I also say thee, That thou art Peter, upon this rock I will build my Church and the gates of hell shall not prevail against it" (Matt. 16:13-20).

Peter's Great Confession

Lord Jesus lauded Peter's spiritual discernment, which made the precious revelation from the heavenly Father possible. And he promised to found His Church on the firm faith Peter had showed, because Peter's great confession that Jesus is the Christ, the Son of living God, showed His unique filial relation to God.

There is no doubt that Jesus' words refer to Peter's manifest faith in the divine Sonship of Jesus. But the word "rock" implies the "Rock of Ages", the title applied to God, meaning "everlasting strength", although the Greek word "Petra" means rock.

Jesus' words, "My Church" with a special emphasis on *my*, signifies that the institution of the Church is a divine one, not a human one. Another important thing about the Church in this passage is that it is identified with the Kingdom of Heaven, for the mention of "gate of hell" indicates "abode of the dead." And the Church is often represented as a city; so here its great adversary "death" is practically represented as a fortified city with walls and gates.

Jesus' promise concerning the Church foretold some distinct basic aspects:

- Faith in Jesus is the key for the fellowship of Christian believers, members of the Church. Their faith binds them together in fellowship not only with the fellow brethren, but also with Jesus as they worship. "For where two or three are gathered together in my name, there am I in the midst of them," said Jesus (Matt. 6:20).

- His promise expressly showed that the Church as an organisation will be indestructible. No amount of perpetuation, nor assaults from Satan from within or without shall destroy the institution of the Church, because the life that is in it is of the Christ.

- The individual members of the Church, united to Christ, shared His indestructible (eternal) life. They shall not be held by the power of death, nor overcome by judgment, but be made, "partakers of the inheritance of the saints in light."

Church and Its Growth

The founding of the first Church of Christ came as yet another landmark in Jerusalem after the Resurrection and Ascension of Lord Jesus Christ. The first Church was founded on the day of Pentecost (50th day) in Jerusalem with the falling of the Holy Spirit on the apostles and Christian devotees. This event took place as foretold by resurrected Christ.

The book of Acts of Apostles in the New Testament gives a thrilling account of this divine event:

> And when the day of Pentecost was fully come, they were all with one accord in one place. And suddenly there came a sound from heaven as of a rushing mighty wind, and it filled all the house where they were sitting. And there appeared unto them cloven tongues like as of fire, and it sat upon each of them. And they were all filled with the Holy Ghost, and began to speak with other tongues, as the Spirit gave them utterance (Acts 2:1-4)

This event marked the foundation of the first Church of 120 men and women; the prophecy made by Joel (2:28) was fulfilled. And Peter stood and gave his first sermon. "Then they that gladly received his word were baptised; and the same day there were unto them about three thousand souls" (Acts 2:41). And chapter 6, verse 7 further tells how there was addition to this number daily. It says, "And the word of God increased; and the number of the disciples multiplied in Jerusalem greatly; and a great company of the priests were obedient to the faith" (Acts 6:7).

As mentioned earlier, the founding of the Church of Christ came as the new beginning of the Kingdom of Heaven in the life of man after the fall of Adam and Eve. In this context, we are reminded of the conversation Jesus had with the Jewish religious leader, Nicodemus.

Nicodemus had not asked any questions, but Jesus knew what he wanted to know: "If thou art the Messiah, as some of us are inclined to believe, tell us how we must enter the Kingdom of Heaven, which thou hast come to establish and of which thou hast said so much."

Jesus explained to Nicodemus that a new birth (meaning a new heart and new nature) is necessary according to the testimony of the Old Testament prophets, who had emphasised: "I will put my law in their inward parts and with it, in their hearts" (Jer. 31:31-33; Eze. 37:26).

Perhaps, taking this thread from the Old Testament words of God and of Jesus in conversation with Nicodemus, Paul, writing to Corinthians, says: "Ye are our epistle written in our hearts, known and read of all men: For as much as ye are manifestly declared to be the epistle of Christ ministered by us, written not with ink, but with the Spirit of the living God; not in tables of stone, but in fleshy tables of the heart" (2 Cor 3:2-3). And he further adds, "Therefore if any man be in Christ he is a new creature; old things are passed away..." (2 Cor. 5:17).

Church: Family of God

Believers of the Christian faith are adopted as Children of God into His adoption through their faith in Jesus as their Lord and Saviour. For "... as many as received him, to them gave he power to become sons of God, even to them that believe on his name" (John 1:12; 2 Cor. 6:18; Gal. 4:5; Rom. 8:15).

Thus, the adoption in God's family is a free gift and supernatural gift to man from God, inward and spiritual, implanted by the Holy Spirit and dependent for its maintenance on union with Christ. Let us take a look at how this adoption stands:

- This sonship conferred on men depended not on human descent for its origin from Abraham, indicating blood relationship;

- Nor does this divinely conferred sonship depend on the sexual relation of their parents, which is the outcome of the will of flesh;

- Nor could be had, wishing it by human effort.

The Church as the assembly of chosen people of God in the body of Christ has been vested with certain authority. The Resurrected Christ gave this authority to the small groups of His disciples when He appeared "where the disciples were assembled for fear of the Jews, came Jesus and stood in the midst, and... said again, 'Peace be unto you: as my Father hath sent me, even so send I you'... he breathed on them, and saith unto them ...'Whosesoever sins ye remit, they are remitted unto them; and whosesoever sins ye retain, they are retained'" (John 20:19-23).

In one of his letters, Paul alluded the relationship of Jesus to the assembly of the believers as "...the husband is the head of the wife; even as Christ is the head of the church and is the Saviour of the body" (Eph. 5:23). And a verse in another letter by the apostle adds the reason: He is "...the beginning, the firstborn from the dead; that in all things he might have the preeminence" (Col. 1:18).

The members of the Church are bound by spiritual relationship with one another. Saints in heaven and earth are united in brotherhood, which is known as brethren. This gives it a universal dimension. The most precious ministries of Peter and Paul made a substantial contribution to this universality as the book of Acts shows.

Although the first Church in Jerusalem was dominated by Jew converts to the Christian faith, beginning with Cornelius, a Gentile from Caesarea, whom Peter baptised along with several others, the first Church became a universal one. It was freed from Judaistic domination, particularly after Saul became Paul, who tirelessly undertook his missionary journeys in the lands beyond the borders of Canaan or Israel in Asia and even Europe, founding Gentile churches, lending truly universal position to the Church of Christ. And now it is encompassing men and women from all over the world, belonging to various cultures, race and colour. So, the Church of Christ now envelops the entire mankind.

God has established the institution of the Church to hold up the truth as a pillar supports a roof, and to keep it unshaken as a firm foundation gives security to building.

Church Is Like Human Body

- "For as we have many members in one body and all members have not the same office: so we being many, are one body in Christ, and every one member one of another" (Rom. 12:-5)

- "For as the body is one, and hath may members, and all the members of that one body, being many, are one body; so also in Christ" (1 Cor. 12:12-13).

- "Wives, submit yourself unto your own husbands, as unto the Lord, for the husband is the head of the wife, even as Christ is the head of the church, and he is the Saviour of the body" (Eph. 5:22-23).

Blessed Family

The Old Testament Book of Psalms gives a beautiful picture of the Christian believer's family life:

> Blessed is every one that feareth the Lord; that walketh in his ways. For thou shalt eat the labour of thine hands: happy shalt thou be, and it shall be well with thee. Thy wife shall be as a fruitful vine by the sides of thine house: thy children like olive plants round about thy table. Behold, that thus shall the man be blessed that feareth the Lord. The Lord shall bless thee out of Zion: and thou shalt see the good of Jerusalem all the days of thy life. Yea, thou shalt see thy children's children, and peace upon Israel. (Ps. 128)

CHAPTER 9

The Word Was Made Flesh

At the end of the introductory passage, John, writer of the fourth Gospel, says: "The Word was made flesh" (John 1:14). Although this is a plain and simple verse, the apostle conveys the most astounding divine fact through it—a fact that changed the entire human destiny! This profound statement of the wondrous fact of Incarnation reveals the central mystery of the Christian faith.

It tells us that God became man (RV: "The Word became flesh") to atone for sin, and to make Christian believers partake of divine nature. And the word "flesh" in this verse means human nature, which consists of body, soul and spirit, without the added idea of "sinfulness."

Let us consider the words of Jesus in the parable or analogy of bread of life: "I am the living bread which came down from heaven; if any man eat of this bread, he shall live forever; and the bread I will give is my flesh, which I will give for the life of the world" (John 6:51).

So, these verses affirm that Redeemer Jesus Christ is "perfect" God and "perfect" man, of a reasonable soul and human flesh subsisting: equal to the Father, as touching His godhead, and inferior to the Father, as touching His manhood. Who although is God and man yet He is not two, but one Christ Jesus.

John declares in his brief but profound preface (John 1:1-14) that:

- The Word was God.
- He was made man.
- He fully and finally revealed the Father in heaven.

This historical fact has been endorsed in the letter to the Hebrews, saying: "God, who at sundry times and in diverse manners spake in time past unto the fathers by the prophets, hath in these last days spoken unto us by his Son, whom he hath appointed heir of all things, by whom also he made the worlds" (Heb. 1:1-2).

Eloquent Messianic Prophecy

The Messianic prophecy Zechariah spoke about smiting of Christ who was fellow with God Himself, saying thus: "Awake, O sword, against my shepherd, and against the man [that is] my fellow, saith the Lord of hosts: smite the shepherd, and the sheep shall be scattered: and I will turn mine hand upon the little ones" (Zech. 13:7).

Who is this "my shepherd" in the above prophecy made by Zechariah; also, who is "my fellow" in this verse? This is how the references to God the Father, God the Son and God the Holy Ghost are scattered throughout the Bible. The triune God constitutes one in three and three in one. When there is one, there are three, and when there are three, there is one. In other words, the addition of God the Father, God the Son and God the Holy Ghost is one and the multiplication is also one.

In the preface of his Gospel, John says, "In the beginning was the Word, and the Word was with God, and the Word was God. The same was in the beginning with God (John 1:1-2). And the Word was made flesh, and dwelt among us, (and we beheld his glory, the glory as of the only begotten of the Father,) full of grace and truth" (John 1:14).

Also, although the Word of God is the "only begotten Son" of God prior to His Incarnation as the "babe Jesus", He pre-existed. The birth of "babe Jesus", His earthly life, public ministry, death on the Cross, Resurrection on the third day from the dead and Ascension constitute the successive milestones on the way of completion of God's glorious Plan of Salvation of mankind. This glorious chain of milestones formed a new beginning for mankind after the fall in the Garden of Eden.

The torn curtain between the Holy and the Holy of Holy in the sanctuary opens the way to reconciliation with God through faith in the Resurrected Christ.

Dwelt Among Us

Apostle John says, "And the Word of God was made flesh, and dwelt among us." This literally means that 'the Word of God, the only begotten Son, dwelt in the tabernacles among us", the tabernacle being His (incarnate) body. The words of Jesus Christ while talking to the Jews, confirm this: "Jesus answered and said unto them, destroy this temple and in three days will I raise it up" (See John 2:19; also, 2 Cor. 5: 1,4; 2 Peter 1:13-14).

How is Jesus a true man? Let us try answering this question.

- He possessed true human soul, for He himself said: "I am the good shepherd; the good shepherd giveth his life for the sheep" (John 10:11).

- He hungered and was thirsty (Luke 4:2; John 4:7).

- Jesus said: "I lay my life that I might take it again" (John 10:17; also, 12:37).

- He possessed a human spirit; he was in real sympathy because he was a "man of sorrows." When Jesus therefore, saw her weeping and the Jews also weeping, which came with her, he groaned in the spirit, and was troubled (John 11:33 and 12:27).

- He was subject to painful human experience: He was weary, (John 4:6); He wept. (John 11:35).

Thus, John emphasises the unity of Jesus' person and the unbroken stream of his consciousness, reaching back beyond Incarnation into eternity (John 1:1, 3:13, 6:33, 38, 41-42, 50-51, 58; and 17:5).

Cross at Calvary

Jesus' incarnation with definite death on the Cross at Calvary was in accordance with the divine Plan of Salvation of mankind. Jesus Christ, the only begotten of the Father, became the son of man. He sacrificed His life on the Cross as the representative of mankind: Because sin-suffering teaches that communication with God has been broken and that access to God can be reopened by the shedding of lifeblood (Lev. 17:11), symbolising expiation and cleansing. So the New Covenant by Jesus was necessary (Lev. 14:11).

Jesus instituted Lord's Supper so as to restore man's broken communication with God (Matt. 26:28; Mark 14:24; Luke 22:19 and 1 Cor. 11:25).

Jesus' sacrifice of Atonement is perfect and once for all. As a background to Christ's unique sacrifice in Atonement on the Cross, we may note that the ritual of the Day of Atonement has been described in the 6th chapter of Leviticus, and they used to take place once a year in the Jewish month of *Tishri* (September). But the sacrifices and purification were occasional and personal, meant to be performed yearly for the nation as a whole, including the priesthood itself, sanctuary and its parts from defilement of the sins of the sins of the people (Also, see Lev. 23:26-32; Num. 29:7-11; Exod. 30:10).

All these conceptions are realised completely in Jesus Christ's self-sacrificing as displayed in the New Testament. Paul records the account of the institution of the Lord's Supper:

> For I have received of the Lord that which also I delivered unto you, that the Lord Jesus the [same] night in which he was betrayed took bread: And when he had given thanks, he brake [it,] and said, Take, eat: this is my body, which is broken for you: this do in remembrance of me. After the same manner also [he took] the cup, when he had supped, saying, this cup is the new testament in my blood: this do ye, as oft as ye drink [it,] in remembrance of me. For as often as ye eat this bread, and drink [this] cup, ye do shew the Lord's death till he come. (1 Cor. 11:23-26).

Parallel to Passover Feast

Just as Jesus is the giver of "living water" so he is the "living bread" or "manna" of the soul. The nearest parallel to this is the Jewish Passover (feast). Some of the hearers of Lord Jesus had heard the Baptist call Him "the Lamb of God" that taketh away the sin of the world. As the blood of the Pascal Lamb had protected the Israelites of old from the sword of the destroying angel so the death of the Lamb of God would give spiritual life to the whole world.

The "flesh" of Christ means His human nature—and His blood, His Atoning blood, shed for the sins of the world. There is a reference to Incarnation and Atonement. The eating and drinking of Christ's flesh and blood is spiritual and can take place only through the medium of faith. In fact, it is the reward of faith. He is in them a spiritual principle of spiritual life and of resurrection; He strengthens their souls, so that they neither hunger nor thirst until they attain everlasting life (John 6:26-59).

The Lord's Supper is ordained as the ordinary and covenanted means of feeding upon Christ—of eating His flesh and drinking His Blood, then onwards by the apostles, practiced in the early Churches in Jerusalem and several other newly planted churches elsewhere in Europe and Asia.

This vital spiritual union between Christ and Christian believers is illustrated in a parable narrated by the Saviour Himself—the Parable of the True Vine (John 15:1-8)—and by Paul's metaphor of the body of Christ—the Church and the members, Christ and the believers (1 Cor. 12:12f).

CHAPTER 10

What Is Thy Destiny?

The only goal of man should be the attainment of the original human dignity that God gave Adam and Eve when He made them. The dignity of man lay in his freedom to choose. The inability of Adam and Eve to make the right choice turned mankind into a fallen race, ushering in death—both carnal and spiritual.

But God's undying love for man brought hope to the fallen humanity through His redemption plan. In fullness of time, he sent His only begotten Son Jesus to die a sacrificial death on the Cross at Calvary in atonement for the sins of the world. As promised in the Bible, the Messiah, the anointed one, eventually came to the world as the Son of Man.

God Is Love

As pre-destined, Jesus came and gave the great command: "All power is given unto me in heaven and in earth. Go ye therefore, and teach all nations, baptizing them in the name of the Father, and of the Son, and of the Holy Ghost: Teaching them to observe all things whatsoever I have commanded you: and, lo, I am with you always, even unto the end of the world" (Matt. 28:18-20).

Significantly, Jesus promised His followers during His earthly sojourn that He would come back to take them with Him to live in His mansion. The following verse in the Gospel of St. John reveals God's love for mankind: "God so loved the world that he gave his only begotten Son, that whosoever believeth in him, should not perish, but have everlasting life" (John 3:16).

In olden times, God revealed Himself to the fathers of the chosen people of Israel by the prophets, but the revelation was always partial. He finally gave a direct revelation in the person of His Son, Jesus Christ: "God, who at sundry times and in diverse manners spoke in time past unto the fathers by the prophets, hath in these last days spoken unto us by His Son, whom He hath appointed heir of all things, by whom also He made the worlds" (Heb. 1:1-2)

The Second Coming

It was upon the mount of Olives that Jesus spoke to his disciples when they privately asked about the signs of the end of the world and His second coming: He cautioned them against the anti-Christ, so that they may not be deceived by many. He also spoke about the turmoil in the world and persecution of His believers. He explained how inequity would abound and the love of many would wax cold, and the Gospel of the Kingdom would be preached in all the world for a witness to all nations; and then the end would come (Matt. 24:1-14).

When Jesus told the Parable of the Fig Tree, He said: "So likewise ye, when ye shall see all these things, know that it is near, even at the doors... Heaven and earth shall pass away, but my words shall not pass away. But of that day and hour knoweth no man, no, not the angels of heaven, but my Father only" (Matt. 24:33-36).

While cautioning His disciples against getting mislead about Jesus' presence at the time of his second coming, He said: "These things I have spoken unto you, that in me ye might have peace. In the world ye shall have tribulation: but be of good cheer; I have overcome the world" (John 16:33). Thus, these words assure man of his victory over the world through Jesus.

Let us take a look at the secret about the way the human body undergoes a change in the state of "rapture." Paul shared it with the Corinthians, saying: 'Some man will say, how are the dead raised up? and with what body do they come?(1 Cor. 15:35) Howbeit that was not the first which is the spiritual, but that which is natural; and afterward that which is spiritual (1 Cor. 15:46). And as we have borne the image of the earthy, we shall also bear the image of the heavenly" (1 Cor. 15:49).

'Now this I say, brethren, that flesh and blood cannot inherit the kingdom of God; neither doth corruption inherit incorruption...but we shall all be changed (1 Cor. 15:50-51). In a moment, in the twinkling of an eye, at the last trump: for the trumpet shall sound, and the dead shall be raised incorruptible...and this mortal shall have put on immortality, then shall be brought to pass the saying that is written, Death is swallowed up in the victory. O death, where is thy sting? O grave, where is thy victory? The sting of death is sin; and the strength of sin is the law. But thanks be to God who giveth us the victory through our Lord Jesus Christ (1 Cor. 15:50-57).

Test of Worthiness

It is clear that God abdicated a portion of His omnipotence when he gave man the liberty of choice. Man—according to the second chapter of Genesis and our hypothesis—possesses real independence, willed by God, which becomes, in the human species, a tool of selection.

"It is no longer the strongest, the most agile, and the fittest physically who must survive, but the best, the most evolved morally. The new supremacy can only manifest itself if man is free to choose his path. This is, therefore, an apparent limitation of the omnipotence of the Creator, consent to by Him in order to bestow freedom upon the chosen species (of man), so as to impose a final test.

Having been endorsed with conscience, man has acquired an independency of which he must show himself to be worthy, under pain of regressing towards the beast (carnal nature)." (Adapted from *Human Destiny* by Lecomte du Nouy, The New American Library of World Literature Inc., 245, Fifth Avenue, New York, 16, New York, USA. The brackets have been inserted by the author.)

Man's Final Liberation
John has noted an unearthly scene of a new heaven, a new earth and God's people:

> And I saw a new heaven and new earth: for the first heaven and the first earth were passed away; and there was no more sea. And I John saw the holy city, New Jerusalem, coming down from God out of heaven, prepared as a bride adorned for her husband (Rev. 21:1-2).

> And I heard a great voice out of heaven saying, Behold, the tabernacle of God is with man, and he will dwell with them, and they shall be his people and God himself shall be with them and be their God (Rev. 21:3)

> And God shall wipe away all tears from their eyes; and there shall be no more death, neither sorrow, nor crying neither shall there be any more pain: for the former things are passed away... He that overcometh shall inherit all things: and I will be his God, and he shall be my son (Rev. 21:4 & 7).

Man's Limited Expectations

Rabindranath Tagore expresses his expectation and thoughts concerning "heaven of freedom" in one of his poems in *Gitanjali*:

> Where the mind is without fear and the head is high;
> Where knowledge is free;
> Where the world has not been broken up into
> Fragments by narrow domestic wall,
> Where words come from depth of truth;
> Where tireless striving stretches its arms towards perfection;
> Where the clear stream of reason
> has not lost its way into the dreary desert sand of dead habit;
> Where the mind is led forward by thee into ever-widening thought and action—
> Into that heaven of freedom, my father, let my country awake!

—From Gitanjali by Rabindranath Tagore

The Word of God, however, notes the following words of Jehovah God:

> Seek ye the Lord while he may be found, call ye upon him while he is near... For my thoughts are not your thoughts, neither are your ways my ways, saith the Lord. For as the heavens are higher than the earth, so are my ways higher than your ways and my thoughts than your thoughts (Isa. 55:6 and 8-9).

New Heaven

John records yet another scene in "Paradise Restored", which is reminiscent of the Garden of Eden, the river and tree of life, and so on:

> And he shewed me a pure river of water of life, clear as crystal, proceeding out of the throne of God and of the

Lamb. In the midst of the street of it, and on the either side of the river, was there the tree of life, which bare twelve manner of fruits, and yielded her fruit every month: and the leaves of the tree were for the healing of the nations (Rev. 22:1).

And there shall be no more curses: but the throne of God and the Lamb shall be in it; and his servants shall serve him: and they shall see his face; and his name shall be in their foreheads. And there shall be no night there; and they need no candle, neither light of the sun; for the Lord God giveth them light: and they shall reign for ever and ever (Rev. 22:3-5)

Behold, I come quickly: blessed is he that keepeth the sayings of the prophecy of this book. And I John saw these things, and heard them. And when I had heard and seen, I fell down to worship before the feet of the angel which shewed these things. (Rev. 22:7-8)

I Jesus have sent mine angel to testify unto you these things in the churches. I am the root and the offspring of David and the bright and morning star... And let him that heareth say, Come. And let him that is athirst come. And whosoever will, let him take the water of life freely (Rev. 22:16-17).

CHAPTER 11

Know Thy Bible

The Bible is a unique book. It is, in fact, a divine library that unfolds deep spiritual mysteries and leads one and all to the light of life, even eternal life. This great book is divided into two parts, namely the Old Testament and the New Testament. While the Old Testament consists of 39 books, the New Testament consists of 27 books (inclusive of epistles). So, the entire Bible consists of 66 books.

The Bible narrates the wonderful story of the genesis of the world, man and all other living things. Through historical facts, it reveals the works of God and various spiritual mysteries.

The 66 books (See Tables 1-3) of the Old Testament and the New Testament can be divided into seven categories:

- (i)   Historical Books
- (ii) Poetical Books
- (iii) Prophetic Books
- (iv) Gospel Books
- (v)   Acts of Apostles

(vi) Epistles to Churches
(vii) Book of Revelation

Table 1

The Old Testament	
Historical Books	17
Poetical Books	05
Prophetic Books	17
Total	**39**

Table 2

The New Testament	
Gospel Books	04
Acts of Apostles	01
Epistles to Churches	21
Book of Revelation	01
Total	**27**

Table 3

The Bible	
The Old Testament Books	39
The New Testament Books	27
Grand Total	**66**

Cohesiveness of the Sixty-six Books

There is an amazing cohesion in the 66 books of the Bible. Strange as it may seem, it is in the very first chapter of the book of Genesis, the first book of the Bible, that a mention of the trinity of God is made: God the Father, God the Son and God the Holy Ghost. The Old Testament and the New Testament tell us about the triune God—His acts—and the various ways in which the Almighty God reveals Himself to the world. The Bible also reveals various prophecies and God's covenants with man and gives moral codes of conduct so as to guide mankind.

And "when the fullness of time was come" God sent in human flesh and blood His only begotten Son, Lord Jesus Christ, to save mankind through His sacrificial death on the Cross. The prophecies made in regard to the birth of the promised Messiah, His public ministry, His teaching and the fulfilment of God's redemption plan constitute the major part of the New Testament.

However, the last book of the New Testament, i.e., Revelation, tells us about the second coming of our Lord. Broadly speaking, the Old Testament describes the mighty acts of the Lord God Jehovah and the New Testament bears witness to the acts of the Son of God, Lord Jesus Christ; and the "Acts of Apostles" essentially underscore the acts of God the Holy Spirit.

The Holy Spirit is known as the indwelling "Spirit", that is, it "dwells" in believers. The Old Testament Book of Ezekiel talks about the Holy Spirit: "And I will put my spirit within you, and cause you to walk in my statutes, and ye shall keep my judgments, and do them" (Ezek. 36:27). 1 Corinthians also highlights the importance of the Holy Spirit: "Know ye not that ye are the temple of God, and that the Spirit of God dwelled in you?" (1 Cor. 3:16).

How Was the Bible Written?

The Bible was written over a period of 1,400 to 1,800 years by 40 different people living in different places. These writers came from different walks of life. The first five books of the Old Testament were written by Moses, the great servant of God, about 1,400 years before Christ. These books are known as the Pentateuch. The last book of the New Testament, that is, Revelation, was written by John in 100 A.D.

The cohesion of the Bible indicates that this great book was written by only one writer—the Holy Sprit, who inspired all those who wrote it. In other words, it was God who motivated these writers to write the Bible so that mankind could know about Him and His great plan. This is testified by the following two verses:

> Knowing this first, that no prophecy of the scripture is of any private interpretation. For the prophecy came not in old time by the will of man: but holy men of God spake *as they were* moved by the Holy Ghost (2 Peter 1:20-21).

> But continue thou in the things which thou hast learned and hast been assured of, knowing of whom thou hast learned them; And that from a child thou hast known the Holy Scriptures, which are able to make thee wise unto salvation through faith which is in Christ Jesus. All scripture is given by inspiration of God, and is profitable for doctrine, for reproof, for correction, for instruction in righteousness (2 Timothy 3:14-16).

Sum and Substance of the Bible

The biblical verses given below shed useful light on the sum and substance of the Scriptures:

> For God so loved the world, that he gave his only begotten Son, that whosoever believeth in him should not perish, but have everlasting life. (John 3:16)

Then one of them which was a lawyer, asked him a question, tempting Him, and saying, 'Master, which is the great commandment in the Law?' Jesus said unto him, Thou shalt love the Lord thy God with all thy heart, and with all thy soul, and with all thy mind. This is first and great commandment. And the second is like unto it, Thou shalt love thy neighbour as thyself. On these two commandments hang all the law and the prophets (Matt. 22:35-40).

Beloved let us love one another: for love is of God; and every one that loveth is born of God, and knoweth God. He that loveth not knoweth not God; for God is love (I John 4:7-8).

And now abideth faith, hope, charity, these three; but the greatest of these is charity. (1 Cor. 13:13).

Love and charity seem to have vanished from today's materialistic world. Several other verses, like the ones given above, teach us to widen our horizons and help give charity a wider social dimension, which is beyond self and self-love.

Love is the Greatest Gift

Paul wrote to the Corinthians:

Though I speak with the tongues of men and of angels, and have not charity, I am become as sounding brass, or a tinkling cymbal. And though I have the gift of prophecy, and understand all mysteries, and all knowledge; and though I have all faith, so that I could remove mountains, and have not charity, I am nothing. And though I bestow all my goods to feed the poor, and though I give my body to be burned, and have not charity, it profiteth me nothing. Charity suffereth long, and is kind; charity envieth not; charity vaunteth not itself, is not puffed up, Doth not behave itself unseemly, seeketh not her own, is not easily provoked, thinketh no evil; Rejoiceth not in iniquity, but rejoiceth in the truth; Beareth all things, believeth all things, hopeth all things, endureth all things. Charity never faileth: but whether there be prophecies, they shall fail; whether there be tongues, they shall cease; whether there be knowledge, it shall vanish away. For we know in part, and we prophesy in part. But when that which is perfect is come, then that which is in part shall be done away. When I was a child, I spake as a child, I understood as a child, I thought as a child: but when I became a man, I put away childish things. For now we see through a glass, darkly; but then face to face: now I know in part; but then shall I know even as also I am known. And now abideth faith, hope, charity, these three; but the greatest of these is charity (I Cor.13:1-13).

The Apostles' Creed

I believe in God, the Father Almighty, Creator of the heaven and the earth. I believe in Jesus Christ, His only Son, our Lord. He was conceived by the power of the Holy Spirit, and born of the Virgin Mary. He suffered under Pontius Pilate, was crucified, dead and was buried. He descended to the dead. On the third day, He rose again. He ascended into the heaven, and sat at the right hand of the Father. He will come again to judge the living and the dead. I believe in Holy Spirit, the Holy Catholic Church, the communion of saints, the forgiveness of sins, the resurrection of the body and the life everlasting. Amen.

CHAPTER 12

I Will Come Again

Comforting His disciples—just before He was crucified—Jesus said, "Let not be your hearts be trouble: ye believe in God, believe also in me. I go to prepare a place for you ...I will come again and receive you unto myself; that where I am, there ye may be" (John 14:1-3).

The New Testament assures of the Second Coming in unambiguous terms. So the Church of Christ and Christian believers are eagerly waiting for this epoch-making event, for the Second Coming will take the world into the reality of the universal Kingdom of God.

Biblical references to the Second Coming indicate that this great event would take place in two phases:

Phase 1: Secret and Mysterious

Paul describes this mysterious event using the word "rapture" ("being caught up") in regard to Christian believers. He says, '...Behold, I shew you a mystery... we shall all be changed: In a moment, in the twinkling of an eye, at the last trump; for the trumpet shall sound, and the dead shall be raised incorruptible, and we all shall be changed...and this mortal shall have put on immortality, then shall be brought to pass the saying that is written, Death is swallowed up in victory" (1 Cor. 15:51-58).

In the first stage, however, Jesus would not come right back to earth; He would come in a cloud where He would be seen only by His believers; His own words testify to this, saying: "Verily, verily I say unto you, the hour is coming, and now is when the dead shall hear the voice of the Son of God: and they that hear shall live" (John 5:25). It appears that Jesus would come from heaven half-way between the heaven and the earth, so as to take His redeemed people, the Church.

Also, writing to the Thessalonians, Paul goes a step further when he says: "For this...we which are alive and remain unto coming of the Lord shall not prevent them which are asleep, For the Lord Himself shall descend from heaven with a shout, with the voice of the archangel, and with the trump of God, the dead in Christ shall arise first. Then we which are alive and remain shall be caught up together with them in the clouds, to meet the Lord in the air; and so shall we ever be with the Lord. Wherefore comfort one another with these words" (1 Thess. 4:15-18).

Tribulation on Earth

The "rapture" would be followed on earth by an unprecedented trial and tribulations for seven years. For the earth then will be without the Church of Christ, because He will suddenly and unexpectedly call His Church away to be with Him. Those died in Christ would be raised from the dead, i.e., resurrected. And all true believers living at that time would be taken up in the air without knowing physical death.

Consequent on these two most astounding incidents, the world will be left without restraint wrought about by the Church on evil forces; the devil will be hyper-active, knowing his time is short.

Thus the world will experience trials and tribulation for seven years, of which the first half, i.e., three-and-a-half years, will be bearable to some extent, but the second half will be rather unbearable, because the work and ministry of the Holy Spirit will be at the lowest level in the hearts of men and women.

And then shall the wicked one be revealed. The wicked one will wreak unlimited havoc on earth as noted in the second letter to the Thessalonians: "For the mystery of the inequity doth already work: only he now letteth will let, until he be taken out of the way. And then that the Wicked be revealed, whom the Lord consume with the Spirit of His mouth, and shall destroy with the brightness of His coming...And for this cause God shall send them strong delusion, that they should believe the lie: that they all might be damned who believed not the truth, but had the pleasure in unrighteousness" (2 Thess. 2:7-12).

Biblical phrases such as "Blessed Hope" and "great hope of the future" imply the next importance phase in the life of the Church of Christ, which is the body of Christ comprising the believers. Before facing the climactic Crucifixion, Jesus comforts His disciples: "Let not your hearts be troubled; ye believe in God, believe also me. In my Father's house are many mansions; if it were not so, I would have told you, I go to prepare a place for you. And if I go and prepare the place for you, I will come again, and receive you unto myself; that where I am, there ye may be" (John 14:1-3).

Phase 2: Judge with Glory and Authority

In the second phase of Jesus' Second Coming, He will come with His saints in His glory and His full authority. The visible worldwide Kingdom of God will be set up; and under His over-riding control, His redeemed people will rule over all the nations of the world. The Lord will come to the Mount of Olives and, at the same time, many geographical changes will take place in the earth.

Zechariah says: "Then shall the Lord go forth, and fight against those nations, as when He fought in the day of battle. And his feet shall stand in that day upon the mount of Olives, which is before Jerusalem on the east, and the mount of Olives shall cleave in the midst thereof toward the east and toward the west, and there shall be a very great valley: and half of the mountain shall remove toward the north, and half of it toward the south, '(Zech. 14:3-4). And while 14:6-7 tell about "one day", 14:8 adds, saying, "living waters shall go out from Jerusalem." And the book of Revelation specifically says that the literal outflow of some special kind of water will purify the Mediterranean Sea, polluted during the great tribulation (Rev. 8:8-9).

The Old Testament and the New Testament Correlated

The following verses from the Old Testament find fulfilment in the New Testament:

- **Isaiah 9:6-7 :** These verses tell us about the names and origins of "a child" to be born of a Virgin.

- **Deut.30:2-6:** These verses from the Old Testament concern all the essential happenings of Jesus' Second Coming.

- **Daniel 7:13-14:** heses verses see the Second Coming in relation to the Kingdom,

- **Psalms 24, 72, 96 and 110:** These psalms shed light on passages related to the Second Coming.

Acts of Apostles (1:10-11) see the second coming of Lord Jesus Christ in relation to the Kingdom. "Ye men of Galilee, why stand ye gazing into heaven? this same Jesus...shall so come in like manner, as ye have seen Him go into heaven"—these words of the angel show that the same degree of physical and undeniable visibility of Jesus' Second Coming will be experienced by the world as it was witnessed by hundreds of his disciples and followers at the hour of His ascension.

Vast Difference

Jesus is to return to earth in power and glory. It is clearly stated, "The Lord my God shall come, and all saints with Him; these saints are His own people, the Church, in the glorified and resurrected bodies, endowed with the power and divine authority. They will accompany Him in order to play a central part in the setting up of the worldwide Kingdom of God."

Thus, the Second Coming will be a majestic descent, the culminating phase in the history of the earth: Not again will a "babe in a manger" be declared the world's number one ruler. He would no longer walk on earth in submission or humiliation, for He is to dominate the rulers of the world with power and authority, as is stated in the Book of Revelation.

John says: "And I saw heaven opened, and behold, a white horse, and He that sat upon him, was called Faithful and True, and in righteousness He do judge and make war..... His eyes were as a flame of fire, and on His head were many crowns: and He had a name written, that no man knew, but He Himself...And His name is called The Word of God. And the armies which were in...And He hath on His vesture and on His thigh a name written, KING OF KINGS, and LORD OF LORDS." (Rev. 19:11-16)

This present age is demonstrating the evil and corrupting power of sin; the coming age will reveal the glory of God, as the prophet Habakkuk says, "For the earth will be filled with the knowledge of glory of the Lord, as the waters cover the sea" (Hab. 2:14). Every eye shall behold His glory, and every heart shall bow in worship and acknowledgment of His true greatness and goodness.

Second Coming and Jewish People

When Jesus returns to the mount of Olives near Jerusalem, this time, He will be accepted by the Jewish people and they will be restored to divine favour. Zechariah, who was inspired by the Holy Spirit, says, "And I will pour upon the house of David, and upon the inhabitants of Jerusalem, the spirit of grace and of supplications: and they shall look upon me whom they have pierced, and they shall mourn for him, as one mourneth for his only son, and shall be in bitterness for him, as one that is in bitterness for his firstborn" (Zech. 12:10).

The Bible tells the history of the Jewish nation. The Jews are God's chosen people. What we are now witnessing is the physical rebirth of the nation of Israel, which depicts the literal fulfilment of the prophecies made by prophet Ezekiel (chapter 37). The Israelites were scattered throughout the world and were brutally persecuted for rejecting the long-promised Messiah—Lord Jesus Christ at His first advent.

Jesus clearly said about His Second Coming with His saints/Church with a view to setting up His visible and worldwide Kingdom and restoring His chosen, Jewish people. Over 2,600 years ago, God said to them, "Behold, I will gather them out of the countries wither I have driven them, and I will cause them to dwell safely: and they shall be my people, and I will be their God...for thus saith the Lord: Like as I have brought great evil upon this people, so I will upon them all the good that I have promised them" (Jer. 32:37-42).

And finally, as the Jewish people are fully restored, Jerusalem will become the capital of the world. So here we see some of the revelations of God concerning what is going to take place on earth in the future.

Restored In Promised Land

The Independent nation of Israel was established in May 1948, and most of the Jewish people have already returned to their promised land. All this is only a preparation for a greater event in the grand plan of God for His chosen people.

At present, a vast majority of Jews are returning in unbelief. Only a few have real faith in God. And even fewer are actively looking forward to welcoming their Messiah.

Why the Kingdom Failed?

There are two reasons owing to which the previous kingdom in the world failed:

(a) Those who wielded power became corrupt, fallible and, as a result,

made grave mistakes.

(b) Those who served under such rulers or leaders failed too.

However, there will be no such failure in this Kingdom; for it will be ruled by the King of Kings, and the Lord of Lords, and since He is the only begotten Son of God, there will be no such mistakes in His decisions.

He will rule over the nations from His capital city Jerusalem. Like Isaiah says: "And many people shall go and say, Come ye, and let us go up to the mountain of the Lord, to the house of the God of Jacob; and he will teach us of his ways, and we will walk in his paths: for out of Zion shall go forth the law, and the word of the Lord from Jerusalem. (Isa. 2:3).

The whole earth will enjoy peace and prosperity, such as never did before. There will be no war, destruction or disobedience; crime and vandalism will be immediately punished. To carry out His will, the Lord will have under Him multitude of tried and tested servants.

End of Empires and Universal Kingdom of God

The Book of Daniel (chapter 2) shows how some of the worldly kingdoms will precede the universal Kingdom of God on earth. This chapter particularly tells us how four Hebrew young men, namely Daniel, Hannania, Mishael and Azriah, firmly rooted in faith in God, helped in establishing His supremacy in the famous and powerful Babylonian empire of king Nebuchadnezzar.

Nebuchadnezzar, in his second year, had a dream. He wanted the wise men of his court describe and interpret it or else they would be slain. The men said that that was beyond their power, but expressed their readiness to explain the dream if the king told them about its nature. But Nebuchadnezzar persisted; he ordered that they should be slain. (Dan. 2:1-13).

Daniel, however, interposed and asked that the execution of the penalty should be delayed. In answer to his prayer and those of his companions, God revealed the dream and its meaning to Daniel, who thanked God for the divine favour. Daniel was then brought before Nebuchadnezzar. After explaining the true source of his knowledge, he proceeded to interpret the dream. (Dan. 2:14-31)

Nebuchadnezzar's Dream

What the king has seen in his dream was a great image with a head of gold, a breast and arms of silver, a belly and thighs of brass, legs of iron and feet of iron mingled with clay. Suddenly, a stone fell on its feet and broke them into fragments; the whole image crumbled into pieces and was carried away by the wind.

The stone then became a great mountain, which filled the whole earth (2:31-35). The head of gold represented Nebuchadnezzar's empire, the part of the image made of silver, brass and iron represented the three kingdoms that should arise (Dan. 2:31-43).

In the days of the end of these events, God would set up a universal and everlasting kingdom. On hearing the interpretation, Nebuchadnezzar acknowledged the greatness of true God and promoted Daniel as governor of the province of Babylon and chief of the wise men. In any interpretation of chapter 2 of the Book of Daniel, the central truth lies in the prophecy of the Kingdom of God, which is to supercede all human empires, and more importantly, the ever-increasing fulfillment of the prophecy in New Testament times.

CHAPTER 13

Did Jesus Exist?

Did Jesus exist? The Bible warns us that such skeptical questions will keep surfacing time and again: "But, beloved, remember ye the words which were spoken before of the apostles of our Lord Jesus Christ; How that they told you there should be mockers in the last time, who should walk after their own ungodly lusts" (Jude 1:17-18).

So it is incumbent upon Christian believers to examine the "secular sources" that help attest the authentic accounts of Jesus' life and works, as given in The New Testament. Let us, therefore, look at Jesus from the perspective of eminent historians, writers and representatives of the ruling authorities of ancient times.

There are several historians, secular writers and representatives of the then ruling class whose writings go a long way towards attesting the truth about the life of Jesus. Let us take a look at them.

Sufficient Evidence
Cornelius Tacitus (A.D. 55-118), Pliny the Younger (A.D. 61-114) and Suetonius (A.D. 69-140) wrote of the events that had

taken place merely thirty years before their birth; moreover, their official positions gave them access to good historical information. The evidence that they give is more than sufficient to establish the actual historical existence of Jesus.

Historian Tacitus

A contemporary of Pliny the Younger, Cornelius Tacitus was the greatest historian of ancient imperial Rome. He lived through the reigns of six Roman Emperors. Scholars acknowledge his "moral integrity" and "essential goodness." Tacitus tells how Christians, who were hated by the populace for their "crimes", were made scapegoats by Emperor Nero for the great fire of Rome (A.D. 64)!

In his *Annals*, Tacitus writes that the name of Christians comes from Christ who was executed in the reign of Emperor Tiberius by the Procurator Pontius Palate; and the pernicious superstitions, suppressed for while, broke out afresh, and spread not only through Judaea, the source of malady, but even throughout Rome itself, "where everything vile comes and is feted."

Titus then refers to the reign of Emperor Nero and the actual presence of Christians in Rome, saying, "But not all relief that could come from a man, not all the bounties that the prince could bestow, nor all the atonements which could be presented to the Gods availed to relieve Nero from infamy of being believed to have ordered conflagration, the fire of Rome. Hence to suppress with the most exquisite tortures, who were hated for their enormities."

It is clear that the patrician Tacitus had no sympathy for Christianity, practiced as it was by the lower classes in general and orientals in particular. Evidence provided by Tacitus is, therefore, all the more valuable. He had the good opportunity to get well-informed about the origin of Christianity, for in A.D. 112, he was governor of Asia, where Christians were numerous.

Excerpts Preserved

Indeed, Tacitus referred to them again in the last book of his Histories of which an excerpt has been preserved. In it, he recognises the fact that Christianity originated as a sect within Judaism though it was by his time quite distinct. And he gives a remarkable piece of information that the Roman general Titus hoped, by destroying the temple at Jerusalem in A.D. 70, to put an end to both Christianity and Judaism, on the theory that if you cut the root, the plant will soon wither.

Writers of the status of Pliny and Tacitus make the historicity of Jesus of Nazareth quite unambiguous.

Earliest Secular Writer—Thallus

How much further can we go back? Is there any first-century witness to Jesus among the pagan writers or historians?

There is an important Christian traveller and historian called Thallus, who wrote in Rome in about A.D. 52. His work is lost, but a fragment of it is preserved in the second-century writer, Julius Africanus, who tells us about the darkness that fell when Jesus died on the Cross (Mark 15:33). Thallus was among the earliest secular writers of history. He wrote around A.D. 52 a book of history of the Eastern Mediterranean world, from the Trojan wars to his own times.

Unfortunately, his writing did not survive, but we have fragments cited by other writers, such as Julius Africanus, who wrote around A.D. 220-221, commenting on the darkness that enveloped the land during the late afternoon hours, when Jesus died on the Cross.

Julius Africanus says: "Thallus in Book Three of his history, explains away the darkness as an eclipse of the sun—

unreasonably as it seems to me, because a solar eclipse could not take place at the time of the full moon day, and it was at the season of the full moon that Christ died on the cross."

Full marks to Julius Africanus for his clear objection to Thallus' statement: "You cannot have a total eclipse of the sun when there is full moon, as it was at Passover tide when Jesus died on cross."

It was not only the Cross of Lord Jesus that was familiar to Pagans in the capital in the Fifties (of the first century), so was the story of His resurrection, if we may judge by the probable significance of the following pieces of evidence:

A remarkable piece of an inscription has turned up, belonging to the time of Claudius Caesar, who was the emperor from A.D. 41 to A.D. 54. (This is the latest inscription that can be dated. Some authorities assign it to the reign of Tibberius, A.D. 14 to 38).

In that inscription, Tiberius expresses his displeasure at the report he had heard of the removal of the bodies of the dead from the tomb; and he gives stern warning that any further tampering with graves will incur nothing short of a death penalty.

Of all the places, this inscription was found in the town of Nazareth although it has been curiously neglected by theologians. Roman historians such as Professor Momigliano and Blaiklock regard this very short thread as official reaction to the Governor of Judea's report on the crucifixion of Jesus and its sequel.

In other words, within a decade of the crucifixion of Jesus, the Christian faith was known to the Roman Emperor. One Suetonius, court official under Hadrian and analyst of the Imperial House, records that Claudius expelled the Jews from

Rome, because they were constantly making disturbances at the instigation of Chrestus.

The date, according to Orosius, was A.D. 90. Two of the people involved in this expulsion order were Aquilla and Priscilla, who were Jews by birth, but were Christians by faith or belief (Acts 18:2).

The misspelling of the name Christ as Chrestus was a common error made by pagan writers or historians after the inception of Christianity. It is quite significant to note the reference in this writing to the historical fact that Pontius Pilate ordered the crucifixion of Jesus Christ.

Pliny the Younger

The most interesting account of Christianity comes from the pen of Pliny the Younger. He was sent by Emperor Trajan to govern the province of Bythinia in Northern Turkey in the year A.D. 112. Pliny had a typical bureaucratic mind and wrote letters to his superiors on every conceivable topic—one of these letters concerned Christianity.

In that letter, he says: "Everywhere he went in his province, including villages and country districts, he found Christian believers. Moreover, their rapid spread had assumed the proportion of a major social problem! The Pagan temple had to close down for lack of Customers, the sacred festivals had been discontinued, and the demand for sacrificial animals had ceased."

Clearly, Christianity was very much on the move by the end of the first century, even in so remote a province as this, at the edge of the Roman Empire.

Those who persisted in their faith, he (Pliny) executed; He considered that such men were obviously contumelious and deserved to die. But he confessed that he was perplexed about the nature of their crime. He had discovered from those who recounted, in the face of persecution that no enormities were practised in Christian assemblies.

According to Pliny, the whole guilt of Christians was that they refused to worship the empirical statues and the images of gods (pagan) and were in the habit of meeting on a certain day, that is, probably on Sunday, before it was light, when they sang in alternate verses a hymn to Christ as God.

They took oath (the baptism promise) not to commit crime. Their lives were exemplary: you would not find fraud, adultery, theft or dishonesty in them. At their common meals they did not eat murdered infants (the charge of cannibalism was often made against Christians by ignorant people).

Pliny was perplexed by the apparent harmlessness of all this. Hence his letter to the Roman Emperor (Pliny, Epistles).

Jewish Historian: Josephus

Josephus was a Jew who provided most important Jewish witness to the historicity of Jesus Christ. Josephus (Ben Mattathias, better known in our times as just Josephus), was born around A.D. 38, died after A.D. 100. He was a Jewish aristocrat and a priestly politician.

He was a Jewish historian in the pay of the Romans. He writes that "there was at that time Jesus, a wise man, if it could be lawful to call Him a man, for He was a doer of wonderful works, a teacher of such men as receive the truth with pleasure.

"He drew to him both many of the Jews and many of the Gentiles. He was the Christ, and when Pontius Pilate, at the suggestion of the principal men among us (Jewish community), had condemned Him to death on cross, those that loved Him at the first did not forsake Him, for He appeared to them alive again on the third day as the divine prophets had foretold these and ten thousand other wonderful things concerning Him. And the tribes of Christians, so named from Him, are not extinct at this day."

These writing do not seem like the writings of the orthodox Jew. A Jew who did not believe in Jesus, would not be willing to call him "the Messiah" and to attest to miracles and the resurrection.

Thus, if we assume that the underline portions are in doubt Christian addition, as many scholars would agree, we still have sufficient information. That there lived a person called Jesus, who was a doer of miracles and considered to be a teacher. There is once again the attestation that He died at the hands of Pontius Pilate.

Josephus was one of the commanders in the war with Rome, and after A.D. 70, he set out to re-establish the credit we know that the forth-century historian Eusebius read Josephus' work and quoted it two times, as a reliable source of valuable information about Jesus Christ and Christianity in his own writing.

Josephus is known for two major works: *Antiquities of the Jews* (c. 94) and *The Jewish War* (c. 75). After A.D. 70, he set out to re-establish the credit of Judaism in the minds of the Roman society in general and the Imperial family in particular. Hence his work *Antiquities of the Jews*. He wrote *The Jewish War* in order to inform the Roman public more accurately about the religions of his forefathers, Jews.

This apologetic work naturally kept to the minimum any material that would irritate Roman readers. Nevertheless, we find in it such names as Pontius Pilate, Annas, Caiphas, the Herods, Quirinius, Felix, Festus and several others. Josephus talks about John the Baptist, his preaching, baptising and execution as well.

Jesus-Messiah, says Josephus

Writing about Lord Jesus Christ, Josephus says: "There was at this time Jesus, a wise man, if indeed we should call him a man, for He was a doer of wonderful deeds, a teacher of such men as receive the truth with pleasure.

"Jesus drew over to Him both many of the Jews and many of the Gentiles/ Greeks. He was the Christ (Messiah), and Pontius Pilate, at the suggestion of the principal men among us (Jews), had condemned Him to death on the cross, those that loved him at the first did not forsake Him; for he appeared to them alive again the third day, as the divine prophets had foretold these and ten thousand other wonderful things concerning him.

"And the tribe of Christians so named from him are not extinct at this day."(*Antiquities of Jews* 18:3.3) And what is most significant of all things is the extended reference to Jesus Himself: "And there arose about the time, (A.D. 26-36) that is, when Pontius Pilate was the procurator in Jerusalem. Josephus wrote very highly about Jesus Christ as 'wise man', 'doer of marvelous deeds', 'a teacher of men' and so on."

Most Surprising Testimony

This, of course, is the most surprising testimony coming from someone who was not a Christian believer. These writings do not seem like the writings of an orthodox Jew. A Jew who does not believe in Jesus would certainly not like to regard Jesus as a "Messiah" and to attest to "miracles" and "resurrection." So, there is once again the attestation that Jesus died at the hands of Pontius Pilate.

We, therefore, have every reason to believe that the person named Jesus was not an imaginary or mythological figure, but a person who walked the streets of Palestine–a person whose life disturbed the status-quo.

Eusubius Quotes Josephus

The fourth-century historian Eusubius attached a lot of importance to the manuscripts of Josephus. He quoted it twice: "If indeed we should call him (Lord Jesus) a man" and "this man was the Messiah." The first remark may allude to his divine claims and the second one to the charge affixed to His cross, while the passage about His resurrection may merely be meant to reflect Christian propaganda.

Be that it may, we have in this passage of Josephus a very powerful and independent testimony to the historical reality of Jesus of Nazareth. The stories about Jesus were no myth—as some of the skeptics suggest. They were so circumstantial and so well attested that they found a place in this apologetic work of Josephus.

All the earliest converts to Christianity were, of course, Jews. They obviously formed the majority in the early apostolic churches. Jesus was a Jew, born among the Jews, and many of the Jews believed in Him and, as mentioned above, the early Church was largely Jewish in composition.

But the historical fact remains that Jesus was actually rejected and opposed by His own people or the Jewish community. The most religious and political rulers did not believe in Him. Obviously, most of the Jewish writings do not make flattering references to Jesus. But this is added proof that there was no attempt to create an ethereal persona.

Lucian—the Greek Satirist

Lucian, the Greek satirist of the second century, writes about "the Christians who worship a man to this day—a distinguished personage, who introduced their novel rites and was crucified on that account... You see these misguided creatures start with the general conviction that they are misguided creatures... are immortal for all times, which explains the concepts of death and voluntary self-devotion which are so common among them: and it was impressed upon them by their original law-givers that they are all bothers, from the moment that they are converted, and deny the gods of Greeks/Greece and worship the crucified sage, and live after his laws. All this way they take quite on faith, with the result that they despise all worldly goods alike, regarding them merely as common property!"

The tone of the above passage indicates that there may have been contempt for Jesus and definitely for His followers.

Other References in Jewish Writings

There are many clear references to Jesus and Christianity besides those made by secular historians, such as Josephus. These references are located in the following Jewish writings:

- The Mishnah (The Jewish law code)
- The Talmud (Commentaries on these laws)

The Talmud was an ancient collection of rabbinical laws, law-decisions and comments on the laws of Moses. It also preserves the oral traditions of the Jews.

Passover Eve, Crucifixion of Jesus

The Talmud referring to Jesus as Yeshua says, "It has been taught on the eve of Passover, they hanged (crucified) Yeshua. And an announcer went out ahead of Him, for forty days, (saying): 'He is going to be stoned, because He practiced sorcery (miracles) and enticed and led astray.' And one, who knows anything in His favour, let him come and plead in this behalf. But not having found anything in His favour, they hanged Him on the eve of the Passover." As expected, the data affirm that there was a person named Jesus who was executed by hanging (as crucifications were called in those days).

Unusual Birth Referred

The birth of Jesus was known to be unusual. The Jews knew all about the claims made for Jesus' birth from a virgin (Mary) and from the earliest days (when Jesus was called 'the son of his mother' in Mark 6:3—an unpardonable insult to a Jew), they put a sinister interpretation on it. But even this provides some sort of confirmation of the Christian claim that Jesus' birth was different.

Similar corroboration is found in the sayings of Rabbi Eliezer: "Balaam looked forth and saw that there was a man, born of women, who should rise up and seek to claim himself God, and cause the world to go astray...Give heed that you go not after that man; for it is written, God is not man that he should lie. ...And if he says that he is God, he is a liar, and will deceive and say that he is parting and will come again at the End. He says it but will not perform it."

Such sentiments are characteristic of rabbinical opposition to Christianity. But consider what indirect attestation they afford to the Gospel story! And Jesus is not referred to by name, but it is obviously He who is referred to by "born of a woman" and "seeks to make himself God."

The divine claims of Jesus and his assertion that he would come again at the end of the world are already reflected in the passage as is the recognition that Jesus' purpose embrace the whole world, not the Jews alone.

Pun on the Word Gospel

There is a passage that makes a biting pun on the word "gospel"; another one talks about Jesus' disciples; and yet another one tells us that Jesus performed miracles by means of magic that he had learnt in Egypt.

The Jews never doubted the miracles performed by Jesus, but they attributed them to demonic agencies—as the Pharisees had done in the Gospel: "By the prince of demon he cast out demons" (Mark 3:22). Another passage records his execution: "On the eve of Passover, they hanged Yeshua of Nazareth."

A lot has been said to show that there is some sort of Jewish support for the historicity concerning the following topics:

- Unusual birth of Jesus
- Miracles performed by Jesus
- Messianic claims
- Teachings
- Crucifixion
- Disciples
- Disputed resurrection of Jesus
- The author of Christian faith

Yet another major Jewish evidence is well given by the Jewish writer Josephus Klusner in his book *Jesus of Nazareth*.

Drawing Conclusions from Non-Christian Writings

Edwin Yamauchi, professor of history at Miami University, says that even if we did not have the New Testament, we would be able to conclude after considering the writings of Tacitus, Pliny the Younger, Thallus, Josephus and Eusebius, the Mishnah and the Talmud that:

- Jesus was a Jewish teacher.

- Many people believed and benefited from His physical and spiritual healing—miracles.

- Jesus was rejected by Jewish teachers, religious rulers, etc.

- He was crucified under Pontius Pilate during the reign of Tiberius.

- His disciple and ever-increasing followers believed that He rose from the dead on the third day and is still alive; and Christian faith spread beyond Palestine so that there were multitudes of them in Rome by A.D. 64.

- All kinds of people from the cities and even countryside— men, women, slaves and free ones—worshipped Him as God by the beginning of the 2nd century A.D. (Adapted from the quotation by Cyril Georgeson, *Light of Life*, April 2009).

Dead Sea Scrolls and Essences Sect

The recent discovery of Dead Sea Scrolls from a library hidden in the caves near the Dead Sea in A.D. 68 brought to light an ascetic community that produced them. This community was wiped out by the invading Roman legions who destroyed the Temple of the Jews and even Jerusalem city.

This Jewish community is identified with the Essence Sect of Judaism in the 1st century A. D. It constituted the third great sect along with the Pharisees and the Sadducees, as reported by Philo and Josephus.

But as Prof. Rowley puts it, "The Dead Sea Scrolls and the community which produced them belonged to pre-Christian era or century. They are highly relevant to the background of Christianity... They enrich our knowledge in the preceding couple of centuries..."

From this cursory survey of pagan, secular historians and Jewish evidences related to the rise of Christianity, it is clear that Lord Jesus is no myth. There is no doubt that He really lived and died under the procurator Pontius Pilate during the reign of Tiberius Emperor.

CHAPTER 14

Influence of Christianity

The advent of Jesus Christ proved to be such an impact-making event in human history that it became a distinct line of demarcation in the unceasing flow of time, showing the period Before Christ (B.C.) and the period After Christ (A. D.).

The Bible consisted of only the Old Testament before Jesus' first advent. With the first advent, God continued and completed His own revelation to mankind, adding the New Testament, which included Jesus' life on earth, public ministry, crucifixion, resurrection and ascension to heaven, with the promise of the Second Coming.

Christianity ushered in unprecedented changes in human life. However, satanic efforts partially stifled the Gospel truth for a few centuries, until the medieval age. The Christian world seemed to be groping around in spiritual darkness.

Revival with Protestant Movement

But the Protestant Movement led to the triumph of the Gospel truth in Europe, which rapidly spread throughout the world. Christianity has broken age-old superstitions, spiritual ignorance and meaningless traditions in many parts of the world. It is also involved in supporting human dignity and human rights everywhere.

The Press and Films

Many words and phrases that originated in the Bible have found their way into our English Language newspapers and magazines. For example, "messiah", "His Cross", "crucifying", "bearing one's cross", "eye for eye and tooth for tooth", "baptising" and so on. It is indicative of the indirect influence of Christianity on the print medium.

The influence of the Bible can be seen on Hindi films as well. Biblical expressions such as "messiah" and "God in love" figure in quite a few Hindi films. A person engaged in helping the downtrodden or neglected section of society is often branded as "messiah." Those who suffer are equated with Jesus' Cross. A song in one of the Bollywood films says that "God is an ocean of love."

INFLUENCE OF CHRISTIANITY

No other religion, philosophy, teaching nation, movement—whatever—has so changed the world for the better as Christianity has done.

—Schmidt

The influence of Christianity is not only positive, but also far reaching, despite longstanding ignorance and constant denials of its contribution. The Bible has responded to much of the existing language, literature, fine arts, values, beliefs and practices.

The Christian influence is abundant and well ingrained in today's flourishing societies. It is not enough for a religion to merely establish a doctrine; it must also direct its influences. This is performed by Christianity in the most awe-inspiring and admirable manner.

It may also be noted that the Bible can be used not only as a spiritual guide, but also as a great piece of literature. Some of the literary forms in the Bible are:

- Narratives
- Law
- Genealogies
- Proverbs
- Letters
- Prophecy
- Poetry

The Bible contains some of the best poetry and lyrics ever composed. The most influential book in English literature is surely the Bible. Read the King James Version of the Holy Bible if you want to appreciate the beauty of the English language. William Wordsworth said that poetry is nothing but a spiritual communion between God and the soul of Man. He found the Supreme Being in all the elements of Nature. John Donne, being a staunch Christian, maintained his puritanical spirit and shielded the doctrines of Christianity even in his poetic compositions. John Milton, one of the greatest epic poets ever, showers praise on the Creator. He was of the strong belief that life is a gift from God and that it has to be utilised in the best possible way for the glorification of the Creator and the extension of His Kingdom on earth. William Blake experimented with religious themes and used many biblical ideas. His works embraced the imagination as "the body of God", or "human existence itself." Poets such as Edmund Spencer, Alfred Tennyson, Robert Browning and Robert Frost used many biblical images, symbols and allusions and wove wonderful lines around them. Themes such as the Nativity, the Cross, the Epiphany, Crucifixion, Advent, Resurrection, birth of Christ, the Journey of the Magi, Ash Wednesday, the Holy Trinity, the Second Coming and so on figure prominently in many literary compositions. Modern poets such as T. S. Eliot, Philip Larkin and W. B. Yeats also took up biblical themes and interpreted them in an altogether different manner, which is definitely thought-provoking. Many English plays and novels are based on Christian themes.

Most of these writers believe that we must use our life—our talents and skills—in the best possible way—and nothing in this world is better than God's goodness.

This is beautifully stated by Robert Frost:

The woods are lovely, dark and deep,
But I have promises to keep,
And miles to go before I sleep,
And miles to go before I sleep.

By Dr. Annie John
Lecturer and Head, Dept. of English,
A.R. Burla Women's College, Solapur

IMPACT OF CHRISTIANITY ON PUBLIC LIFE

The impact of Christianity on public life has been remarkable. Consider, for example, an organisation called the Young Men's Christian Association (YMCA). The YMCA movement originally began in England in the nineteenth century. Many young people migrated to London in search of employment. George Williams, a 21-year-old man, knew that these young people without any proper direction in life may get influenced by bad habits and immoral things. So he invited a few young men for bible study and fellowship. Later on, this small group of young men formed YMCA on 6 June 1844. Currently, YMCA has more than 45 million members!

Although YMCAs were founded on Christian principles, they are open to all, regardless of faith, social class, age, or gender. One witnesses the Christian principle of "inclusiveness" at all YMCAs. Through their programmes and activities, YMCAs have helped thousands of young people to change their attitude to life and build their lives. The "C" in "YMCA" has always been expressed directly or indirectly.

Effects of Christianity in India on the Secular World

Christian schools, colleges, hospitals, NGOs and other institutions have been playing an important role in Indian society. The principles of Christian service, leadership and discipline have made a vital impact on the secular world; for example, many hospitals and schools in India prefer to employ Christian doctors, nurses and other paramedical staff and teachers.

Most of our political leaders and social reformers have studied in schools managed by Christians. And many want their children to study or continue studying in educational institutions run by Christians.

Interestingly, Mrs. Sushma Swaraj, Indian politician of the Bharatiya Janata Party and Member of Parliament, preferred her daughter in London to stay at the YMCA Indian Student Hostel.

By Deepak Londhe
General Secretary (C.E.O)
Pune YMCA

*9 7 8 8 1 8 4 6 5 1 5 4 6 *